STE

'Big powers in other-worldly communication
and healing'

Irish News

'Two Worlds at his feet'

Western Mail

'Britain's renowned medium
has helped thousands of people
to contact their loved ones
through his nationwide tours'

HELLO! magazine

'There is no doubting his sincerity
or his honesty'

Girl About Town, London

'Britain's brightest young medium...
Power seems to radiate from his fingertips.
These eyes can see beyond the grave'

Daily Star

'It's hard to be sceptical of the psychic world
when a stranger tells you precisely
what you were doing that morning,
and even days before.
I was startled, almost shocked'

Liverpool Echo

THE SPIRITUAL KEYS
TO THE KINGDOM

A Book of Soul-Guidance for your Life

Books
by the same author:

VISIONS OF ANOTHER WORLD
The Autobiography of a Medium

VOICES FROM HEAVEN
Communion with Another World

IN TOUCH WITH ETERNITY
Contact with Another World

ANGELS BY MY SIDE
The Psychic Life of a Medium

A GIFT OF GOLDEN LIGHT
The Psychic Journeys of a Medium

THE SPIRITUAL KEYS TO THE KINGDOM
A Book of Soul-Guidance for your Life

The Spoken Word
recordings by the same author:

Life After Death
Heal Yourself
4 Meditations
Develop your Mediumship & Psychic Powers
Develop your Healing Powers
4 Visualisations

For details of our Worldwide Internet and
Mail Order Catalogue Service, see page 384

The Spiritual Keys to the Kingdom

Visionary and Poet
Stephen O'Brien

Voices

PO Box 8, Swansea, United Kingdom, SA1 1BL

'THE SPIRITUAL KEYS TO THE KINGDOM'
A VOICES BOOK
ISBN: 0-953-6620-5-5

PRINTING HISTORY:
First Publication of this Original Voices Paperback
in Great Britain in 2002

Typeset by *Voices*.
Front cover photograph of author © Stephen O'Brien
Printed and bound in Great Britain
by Cox & Wyman Ltd.,
Reading, Berkshire.

*Dedicated to all Souls who are marching forward
towards The Light of Perfection and Love.*

*Stephen O'Brien,
'Willowtrees' Cottage,
Wales; July 2002*

Contents

Dedication   7
About the Author   10
'These Am I'   11

How to use
The Spiritual Keys to the Kingdom   13

1 The Voice of your Mind   17
2 The Voice of your Soul   109
3 The Voice of your Spirit   203
4 The Voice of Love   227
5 The Voice of Eternity   343

About the Author

*Stephen O'Brien is a visionary, poet, spiritual
healer, and bestselling psychic author whose work
has helped countless people to find spiritual
knowledge, health and happiness.*

*Through his gift of mediumship he has delivered to
thousands of seekers irrefutable evidence of the
survival of the souls of their loved ones after death.*

*Through his books, educational recordings, media
broadcasts, and via the Internet, his spiritual
teachings have circled the planet and have enriched
millions of lives. He was 47 years old when he wrote*
The Spiritual Keys to the Kingdom.

*The book comprises a treasury of timeless
inspirational guidance that he received over a
number of years from wise discarnate souls; and,
together with his own thoughts, it contains some
passages of great poetic beauty and simplicity.*

*Although he is a quiet unassuming man who lives
in a secluded cottage in Wales, for decades Stephen
O'Brien has toured Great Britain extensively with
his spiritual work.*

*The poem opposite, which is taken from one of his
books,* In Touch with Eternity, *reveals a little more
about his charismatic, yet enigmatic, personality.*

These Am I

I am a speaker of mysteries:
　but the pure in heart
　　glean wisdom, hidden from the wise.

A toucher of souls am I:
　a shaker of death, to life.
　　A lover of the loveless,
　　can moisten tired eyes.
I believe the unbelievable:
　they make my spirit rise.

A stealer of time am I:
　so laugh with me
　and never die.

A Giver of Light I've tried to be:
　shining rays on darkened truths
　and revealing hidden lies.

I've never been a picture on a faded page,
　nor a smiling face
　without a mind to see:
　　and you may know me,
　　if you may know me...

How to Use
The Spiritual Keys to the Kingdom

In this book, you are the Traveller walking along
life's ancient pathway; and as you follow the
road the voices of Angelic Beings of Light and
of your own heart, mind and soul will speak to
you and guide you into right-thinking and right-
action.

But there is another way to use the guidance
herein: at times of stress or anxiety, clasp the
book in your hands and become still for a few
moments.

Calm yourself, and quieten your mind.

When you feel relaxed, be absolutely clear
about what your problem or question is – then
open the book and read the guidance that
presents itself to you.

If at first the help that you need is not plainly
visible, relax and try again – and emerging from
the words on the pages may come a positive
direction or a life-changing thought.

The Spiritual Keys to the Kingdom can be
interpreted in many ways: one can appreciate the
literal meaning of the words on the page, but
there are deeper interpretations, too – meanings
which can be gleaned only by those whose
insight or spiritual awareness has developed to
the point where this inner wisdom can make

itself clear to them.

Each reading may present the seeker with new insights: as your spirituality develops and your consciousness expands, each wise saying may deepen its meaning – and the Kingdom of Heaven, which is the Kingdom of the Spirit, may be revealed to all those who can perceive it.

Some of the themes in these teachings may seem familiar and they will be easy to grasp, but others may seem new and will therefore require further thought and measured consideration. The important spiritual teachings are reiterated in different ways throughout the work.

In essence, this is a guidebook of conduct for your soul; and to make further study of the material easier, I have given each saying its own verse-number, thus: ✧ 12.

Whether you read these inspirational words all in one reading as a narrative or tone poem (from the viewpoint of the Traveller who is walking the Ancient Pathway of Spiritual Light), or dip into them to receive daily guidance, I hope these timeless pearls of wisdom will help you to live a happier, healthier, and more contented life.

Stephen O'Brien

1.

Listen to
The Voice of your Mind…

And the Traveller on the Ancient Pathway lifted up his gaze and saw before him a brilliant star, high up in the bright morning sky, hanging over a great Valley of Light.

"This Guide-Star is The Light of Hope," he said to himself. "And this is The Sacred Valley of Wisdom that our forefathers spoke of in the days of yore. I will move towards it."

And as he did so, the young Traveller remembered all those pilgrims before him who had discovered this revered Valley on their life's journey, and who had been brave enough to stand tall and walk boldly through it; and he recalled the many tales he'd heard around the campfires of how all those who had passed through this place had heard its voices of the spirit, heart, and mind, whispering to their souls.

And he remembered the Old Ones who warned that these voices would guide a Traveller not only into The Light but also into the challenges and thought-provoking ideas that would redirect his feet onto new and innovative roads, roads that would lead to greater realisation and spiritual awareness, and to greater happiness and contentment.

The young Traveller straightened his back: he knew that his walk through the Valley would take him an entire lifetime to complete.

"I will start my journey as a young man and will end it in old age. But am I ready to face this?" he wondered. "Am I willing to relinquish my old ideas and to open my mind to new thoughts?"

He pondered on this for a while... then he stepped into the radiant Valley and strode forward, keeping ever before him the brilliant Light of Hope and waiting to hear the Angelic Beings and the Inspired Voices of his soul speak to him...

As he moved through the verdant grasses and the soft undergrowth he began to think more deeply. "Why am I in this place at this time?" he wondered. "Who am I? And why have I been born into this world?" And from out of a bright Cloud of Light in the azure sky, the gentle tones of the first spiritual voice said:

Who are you?

You are a child of The Living Light.
Every living thing has been created
by The Great Spirit of Life
who dwells within each atom
of every creature,
seen and unseen.

On your journey,
respect The Divine Light
of The Spirit of God
within each living thing,
and treat others
as you yourself would like to be treated –
with kindness and with respect.

In this way lies the road to happiness,
which will help you to become
a more contented and fulfilled being.

Because you have been dreamed into
existence by The Cosmic Mind,
by The Androgynous Spirit,
you are an everlasting part of It.

And on your long journey
through the Earthworld, Traveller,
The Everything has ordained
that you will experience what it means
to be a human being:
you will laugh and you will cry —
you will love and you will hate;
you will fail and you will succeed;
but above all
you will grow.

And you will not leave this world
until all of your lessons
have been learned.

Step forward...

Realise that you belong to
an interconnected community of souls.

We are all part of one nation under God,
and you are a unit of consciousness
which belongs to,
and which has originated from,
this One who is All.

Everyone is your brother and sister —
souls in the animal kingdom
and plants in the world of vegetation
are your kinsfolk
because you are united by
the common motivating
Power of The Spirit,
which is Life Itself.

Every creature is a part of
your intimate family circle;
and if you help and support them,
they will help and support you.

Because you belong to
a Universal Family of Souls
all united under the umbrella
of One Cosmic Father/Mother Soul,
it is right
that you should encourage one another to
progress towards the state of Perfect Love
that your Parent has already attained.

As a Cosmic Being,
realise that you are capable of
many wondrous things.

A Spark of Divine Love
lights up
and ignites
your consciousness and your awareness.

The Power of The All is within you –
and with this God-Power
all things are possible
if you apply yourself diligently
to the tasks in hand.

Although you are not the whole of God –
God is the whole of you.

Your nature is a part of
God's own Nature,
but at present you are unable to register
or to express the totality of God;
only in part
are you able to express His Nature.

But if you reach out to touch His mind,
He will hear your cries,
and His Angels will inspire you to
make the decisions that are best for you.

Realise that you have been born
to live out a life
within the framework of a Divine Plan
which The Supreme Power has formulated
and which is now out-working Itself
through the evolution of all the life-forms
It has created.

We each play out our allotted part
in this Scheme of Eternal Progression,
whether or not we believe
we have freewill.

Because you are a Divine Being
clothed in flesh,
your spirit is eternal
and nothing can ever harm it.

Because you belong to
The Everlasting One,
your Father and Mother
will send a Host of Angels to help you,
if you sincerely request their aid.

Be still,
and listen for the silent voice
within you.

All is One;
and One is All.

The All can be seen
in The One;
and The One can be seen
in The All.

Realise this truth
and The Power of The All
becomes available
to The One.

And the young Traveller marvelled at the
wisdom that was echoing all around him and
within him. And when his mind took flight
and he wondered how he had been formed or
created, The Voice of Nature anticipated his
unspoken question and vibrated the very land
upon which he stood, saying:

You are a triune being
comprising body, mind and spirit:
but these three are not separated,
they are all as One.

Do not abuse these Temples of Light –
take good care of them.

Feed and rest the body
in order to maintain your health,
so that you may live long upon the Earth;
and expand your mental awareness and
sensitivity through observation,
contemplation,
and by questioning everything.

Remember:
you are not a body with a spirit –
you are a spirit
registering through a physical body.

Your personality has been formed
from the countless experiences
that your soul has undergone
through many lifetimes –
and it is not located in your brain
because long after your brain has
decomposed, you will find that your mind
is still alive.

Your spirit is the master,
and your body is the servant.

Take control of your life.

Your body is formed, held together,
and controlled, by your mind.

Your mind is formed by your soul.

Your soul is powered by your spirit.

Your individuality is expressed
through your mind,
and then through your physical
and spiritual bodies.

Your body, mind and spirit
are lit up and empowered by
the precious jewel of conscious awareness,
which comes to you freely from God.

And you can only express outwardly
what is already living within you.

Your body is the Temple of your Spirit
and it is the vehicle of your learning
on Earth,
so keep it healthy and clean,
both inside and out.

Eat no 'dead' flesh;
do not pollute your physical frame
with harmful smoke and fumes;
breathe only fresh pure air;
drink only water that is clean.

Do not harm your body
with toxic drugs and chemicals.

If you eat of death,
death will grow within you.

Feed your body nutritious food:
fresh vegetables, fruits,
grains and pulses,
and the herbs of the field.

Breathe clean air
deeply into your lungs.

Evacuate your body's waste products
regularly.

Take regular exercise
but do not strain or overtax yourself.

Remember that too much activity
is as bad for your health
as too much inactivity is.

Movement and exercise
is good for you.

Your body is a miraculous vehicle:
it is the densest form of Light,
materialised,
and it was created for
movement and repose.

But do not jeopardise your health
by disordering the rhythm of your body:
balance your physical activities
with your mental ones,
and your body and mind
will align themselves with
health and wellbeing.

Exercise moderation
in all things,
and do nothing to excess.

Remember that the maintenance
of your physical frame
is your responsibility.

Your health and wellbeing
is not the responsibility of your doctors
or your therapists;
they are merely there
to advise and treat you.

Your health is your own responsibility.

Your mind has created your body,
and your mind can affect
your body's functions
and its appearance,
for your body is a reflection of
what is living within your mind.

The real you can be seen in
your eyes, in your features, in your
movement, and heard in your voice.

Have a great zest for life,
but always meet the needs of
your physical frame,
and never harm it.

Although your spirit needs no rest,
remember that its casket
must continuously replenish
its energy-reserves.

Do not allow your bloodstream to slow up
through laziness
or a lack of exercise.

Keep the Temple of your Spirit
in good working order,
for if you allow its magnetic
and spiritual forces
to become unbalanced and unwell,
how can you hope to help yourself
or others?

To make your body, mind and spirit
much stronger,
breathe in The Breath of Life.

Breathe deeply,
and not shallowly.

Fill your lungs
with The Power of Life,
and feed your inner vehicles of expression
with the hidden cosmic energies
contained in the air.

Breathe correctly
and your depressions may lift,
your thinking may become clearer,
your ideas may move more quickly
through your mind,
and the answers to your questions
may occur to you more readily.

Traveller,
you must always make time to relax
and to recuperate your energies.

Do not overstrain the physical body,
the emotions or the mind —
be sensible
and give them adequate rest.

Your duties will wait for you.

All work and no play
will unbalance the delicate harmony
of your body,
mind and spirit.

You must recharge your batteries
regularly.

Refresh your mind with repose,
and tomorrow,
when you feel regenerated,
the world will seem a much better place
in which to live.

Obtain adequate sleep.

By all means
sleep on your problems,
and instruct your mind to solve them
for you while you are resting.

Trust
that this will occur,
and when you wake in the morning
the solutions
may become clearer to you.

You can find the answers
to all of your questions
by withdrawing
from the clamour of the world,
stilling your mind,
and carefully thinking over the events
that have brought you to an impasse.

In the silence,
while your body is resting,
your thoughts may gently lead you
to understand
why you are
where you are,
and why whatever has happened to you
has occurred.

To obtain peace of mind,
perfect health, stability,
and a deeper sense of contentment,
you must establish harmony in your life.

Dis-ease stems from a lack of attunement
within the individual.

Put yourself in harmony with
your surroundings, your relationships,
your thoughts and your feelings.

Achieve a harmonious concord
with all things around you
and within you,
and health and peace
will be yours.

Health is a treasured prize that cannot be
taken by force or bought for gold –
it must be earned;
it must be attained;
and then it must be carefully maintained.

There is not one of you who can say,
"I will escape pain and fear;
I will cheat anger and despair,"
for all creatures
will taste these experiences
without exception.

Soul-testing challenges
will occur time and again in your life
until you have learned the spiritual
lessons they came to teach you.

Once you have gained mastery
and control over your Self,
these tests will depart peacefully
and will not trouble you again.

The battles that rage within your mind
and soul can cause great disturbances
within your aura,
within your subtle psychic energy-fields
and your etheric power-gateways that link
up your finer spiritual bodies,
which can then upset your sense of
wellbeing.

Calm yourself.

Make peace with yourself
and with your neighbours;
and resolve to end the battles
that rage within you.

The human race is in pain
because man is constantly at war
with himself.

Do not be fearful of
expressing your emotions.

Everyone should shed a few tears
now and then,
but not too often, and not too intensely.

To cry is healthy:
gentle sobbing
can release your pent-up pain
and your anxieties.

Shedding tears
can cleanse your emotions
and ease your bodily tensions.

Know that you have within you
the power to conquer pain
and to achieve peace –
all you need is the willingness to attain it
and the dogged determination
to formulate,
and then to put into practice,
a sensible plan of action.

And when the young Traveller realised that these mystical voices, which seemed to be emanating from within the very atmosphere of the Valley, were communicating easily with his mind, and that they could read his thoughts – he was troubled.

He halted and, for a while, was unsure of how to proceed.

He began thinking about the nature of his mind and how it had come to into being, and a calm voice said:

Your mind can span endless time
and space,
though it seems quite limited to you
in your present form.

If you truly quieten your thoughts,
and truly still your mind
and just allow yourself to relax,
the answers to all of your questions
will float into your consciousness
without any effort from yourself.

Your thoughts are living things:
they are real energies –
and energy cannot be destroyed.

Like the surface of a calm pond that is
disturbed when a pebble is dropped into it,
your thoughts radiate outwards
like water-ripples.

You cannot isolate your thoughts,
for once they are born
they are instantaneously transmitted
to others.

Therefore, send out only good thoughts,
and you will swell The Reservoir of Love
within the Universe.

And keep this Universal Law
always in mind:
you alone are fully responsible
for your thoughts and actions.

And you alone
will be held accountable for them.

Your thoughts are like boomerangs —
made up of living energy they travel out
into the vast dome-like structure
of the Universe,
gathering speed and momentum
as they go.

On their journey they are often 'caught'
by the minds of other beings
who then add their own energies to them,
their own positive or negative forces,
after which they propel them
on their way again.

Be careful of what you think,
because your thoughts will return to you
in the future.

Traveller, beware!

The thought is the deed:
think it, and truly believe it –
and it shall be.

If only you could see the amazing effects,
for good or ill,
that your words and thoughts
have on others around you
in this world
(and in the next)
you would never feel powerless
or unimportant.

You are fulfilling a unique spiritual role
in The Mystery of Life and Evolution.

Recognise that your mind is a capacity,
a reservoir of thoughts,
and that if you collect these powers
together – you can achieve anything,
provided that you truly believe
in your ability
to materialise your desires.

Thoughts are immensely powerful
energies.

Guard your thoughts well,
for whatever you think of today
will certainly affect the quality of your life
tomorrow.

It may take a thousand years
or several lifetimes
for your thoughts to wing their way
back to you,
but back they will most assuredly come –
for as you sow,
so shall you reap.

Everything you think, say, or do
creates an outcome that can either
be helpful or obstructive:
your thoughts can either
heal or destroy.

What kind of thinker are you?

What kind of healer are you?

Because your thoughts and feelings
are very real energies –
do not curse.

Send out only good thoughts,
and only good thoughts
will return to you;
for those who serve
are served in return.

Grant power only to your constructive,
loving and helpful thoughts –
and express them carefully.

If you allow your mind unbridled freedom,
you place yourself in danger
of being 'controlled'
by waves of undisciplined emotion,
the mighty tides of which
can often bring chaos and disharmony
in their wake.

Always think positively,
and act likewise.

Keep cheerful,
and try to be optimistic.

Take positive thought.

Whatever your goal is in life,
persevere until you achieve it –
don't give up.

In converting positive thought
into positive action,
you will set into motion
positive forces that will help you
to achieve positive results.

Every significant action in
the visible world
is strengthened by souls in
the invisible world.

To achieve success,
keep this thought-affirmation
firmly in your mind:

"I will keep on
keeping on,
and I will get there in the end."

Because of the Universal Law of
Like Attracts Like,
your positive thoughts
will always draw to you the help
and guidance of positive-thinking minds
who live either in this world
or in the next.

But if you succumb to feelings of
insecurity, negativity or doubt,
or depressing ideas of failure,
you will surely seal your fate.

Banish all negative thought
from your mind.

Negative thoughts and actions
will attract to you
negative thoughts and actions.

Keep cheerful
and you will map out for yourself
a much brighter,
clearer, and happier pathway.

Voyager:
you ask why and how
your conditions of life
have been brought about?

The answer is simple:
your past thoughts,
actions, and feelings
have placed you where you are today.

The same energies that you projected
into the ether
are now returning to you.

Your present
is the result of your past.

Your future will be the result
of your present.

Use your mind to look at your life afresh,
but see it with the eyes of your spirit.

Observe your circumstances
from a different viewpoint.

But remember that if you choose
to remain spiritually blind,
you should forgo the right to lead others;
for when the blind
lead the blind
they will both surely fall.

If you want your future to be brighter,
then you must think bright thoughts
and perform kind deeds today.

Waste no more time:
change your thought-patterns now –
for what goes around,
comes around.

Divine Justice operates in this Universe,
and none can cheat it.

He who believes himself
to be of great importance on Earth
may well be the poorest in mind
in The Spirit Realms,
and he will discover that his behaviour
and his thoughts will relegate him
to a lower sphere of existence
in the World of Eternity.

And the first shall be last,
and the last shall be first.

And know that whenever you make
an important decision,
The Great Spirit within you
is fully aware of your choosing,
for His Will is Omnipotent
and it influences the lives of all creatures.

Remember also that The Great Power
has a Darker Side to Its Nature,
just as you have.

We are but pale reflections
of our Creator's Omnipresent Mind.

And as you travel along life's road,
thinking and deciding
where your next steps should be,
use your mind to its full potential.

Do not remain in ignorance.

Learn as much as you can.
Ignorance is not bliss.
Ask, read, look; see;
study, search, investigate.

Knowledge is Power.

Think deeply
about all things.

Accept little at its face value —
question everything.

Do not be gullible:
carefully reassess the facts.

Faith is of no use if it is blind.
Add knowledge to your faith,
and you will give it eyes
to see the truth.

An unquestioning belief
places you in a spiritually stagnant state.

Life is all about movement and change,
progression and development.

Replace your blind faith
with a faith that is based on knowledge.

And do not allow your mind to wallow in
your past glories,
hurts, guilts, or regrets.

Although your memories
can highlight for you
where you may have previously
made mistakes,
you must live for this moment.

Do not wish your life away
with thoughts of what might have been.

Seize the day,
and do not make the same mistakes again.

Everyone needs a goal in life;
something to aim for,
something to achieve.

It is good to dream a dream.

But which is the dream
and which is the reality?

It is all reality
to you, the perceiver...

And as the Traveller progressed along the Path
he grew stronger. He moved into vibrant
adulthood and felt the Pulse of Life coursing
through his veins; and his mind and personality
expanded, and he became more thoughtful.

It was then that he began to seek a purposeful
direction in his life; and he pondered deeply on
this as he stepped further into the midst of the
Valley.

And just when the skies darkened and he
thought he might be lost, he glimpsed again the
constant Guide-Star – and from out of the air,
within the spiritual energy-fields above his
head, the tones of a clear voice reassured him,
saying:

No one is ever lost.

You the captain of your own ship:
aided by wiser minds than your own
you chose your ship
and charted your arduous course,
before you were born into the Earthworld.

There are reasons for everything that
has occurred in your life;
try to discover them —
think more deeply.

Pray.

But remember that your life
is your own ship,
and you should not look to others
to steer it.

When mapping out a new course,
try to broaden your thoughts.

Small-thinking stems from a lack of use
of your reasoning power.

Exercise your mind.
Reassess the situation.

But remember:
because you are never in possession
of every piece of knowledge,
your judgements are often flawed.

Avoid bigotry and narrow-mindedness.
Bigotry gives birth to strife, disharmony,
war and racism.
The bigot hurts himself more than others,
for whatever he thinks of others
and does to them,
will eventually be thought of him,
and be done to him: that is the Law.

You were given a mind to use it,
not to let it slacken
and fall into laziness and confusion.

Do not think or behave like a child.

When you were a child
your understanding was limited.

Now that you are older
you should know better.

A child does not possess
a full awareness of its responsibilities
in the world,
but an adult should.

Seeker:
use your Divine Gift of Intelligence
and you will view more clearly
the bend in the road that lies ahead.

Come what may, you must fulfil
all of your responsibilities.

Do not shirk them:
they are given to you so that your
spiritual understanding may grow
from the experience of
discharging these commitments.

Never be lazy —
think.

Your understanding will deepen
only when you reflect upon
the whys and wherefores
of each situation.

Analyse the causes of your difficulties
and you will unlock
and fling open wide
the doors to success.

Wayfarer,
do not neglect the development of your
mental powers or the expansion of your
Gift of Awareness.

Those who rush through life unaware of
what is happening around them
and, more importantly, within them,
often subject themselves
to crippling stress and deep anxiety.

Insensitive people are frequently shocked
when 'unexpected' events
generate powerful waves of emotion
which sweep them off their feet
and make their lives miserable.

Be sensitive.

You will automatically develop
your soul-sensitivity when you expand
your thinking-processes
and increase the love in your heart.

If you become more aware of your
thought-patterns
and learn to control them —
and forbid them to take control of you —
you will become their master
and they will become your servants.

Then Reason will rule supreme.

Although it is said you cannot reason
with an unreasonable person —
you can try.

Talk over your problems with others.

Sit around a table
with your brothers and sisters
and resolve your differences amicably
and fairly.

Try not to resort to violence.

Avoid war and bloodshed.

Do not split up families
or set people or nations
against one another.

Use tact,
and utilise your reasoning-faculty
to the full.

Work out your goals,
and then pursue them with commitment
and dedication
until you reach them.

Now ask yourself this question:

"What am I doing with my life?
Am I giving enough service to others?
Am I kind enough,
thoughtful and considerate enough
in my dealings with other souls?"

Seeker:
examine your thoughts,
and question your motives.

And once in a while
on your arduous journey through life,
take time to give your mind
a good spring-cleaning.

Take a cool, objective look at
the state of your character
and your spiritual progression.

Draw up an honest
and comprehensive list of
your spiritual debits and credits,
and then determine how to balance them
sensibly.

Think about what you can do
to alleviate much of your stress
and to build up happiness around you.

Look again at your circumstances
and try to perceive them in a new light,
from a different perspective.

Check all the facts again.

Then make a decision,
and act on it.

Say what you mean
and mean what you say.

If you say it – mean it.

And if you mean it – say it.

And if you examine your life
and discover an exciting new direction:
be cautious.

Try to look beyond the obvious.
Make a thorough
and intelligent appraisal
of all the information before you
make any choices.

Those who do not take
sufficient thought
often suffer from the effects of
their hasty actions and words.

And ponder also on this:
are you, in your self-righteousness,
truly aware of your deepest thoughts?

No, you are not.

Then do not chide others
along the pathway,
because it is extremely difficult for you
to judge accurately
another person's motivation.

None of us has the wisdom or experience
to direct another soul's life.

Because you can never see every situation
from its multifarious viewpoints:
think twice
before you give advice.

And here is a further caution:
would you take the advice
that you are prepared to give
so freely to others?

But at all times
throughout your life
keep an open mind,
and try not to be cynical.

Remember that an open mind
can see the way ahead
more clearly than a closed mind can.

Endeavour to strike a fair balance
between the powers of your head
and the powers of your heart;
between the intelligence in your mind, and
the feelings in your heart.

And keep your thoughts in check.

When thoughts gallop away like
wild stallions,
they must be reined in.

And whenever you feel miserable
or dejected – remove yourself from
your present circumstances
and do something different.

Go out.
Taste new experiences.

Encourage yourself to meet others:
visit new groups;
see new places, meet new people;
and the sun will soon shine for you
again.

And whenever you feel irritable or
ill-at-ease — calm down.

Relax.

Whatever has happened to you is not
unique: down through the centuries,
millions of souls
have undergone similar experiences
and have survived them.

Your mind will make you survive yours.

Don't turn your life into a nightmare:
quieten your thoughts and emotions —
and look again.

Things are never as bad
as they at first might seem.

And do not steep your mind in depression,
confusion, or scepticism –
take counsel with wiser souls.

Seek help from others to spark your own
intellect into action
and, from somewhere,
the inspiration that you need
will be forthcoming.

Never abandon yourself
to the way of the dullard,
to the way of the lazy person
who does not, or will not,
think for himself.

And never burden yourself
by carrying in your mind and heart
the weight of bad feelings
you hold against others.

The pressure of negative thoughts on
your brain, and of angry feelings on your
astral body, can make you feel ill.

Make peace with those
who you think may have wronged you,
and start a new day
with a clean mind.

Traveller:
realise that no one is perfect,
and recognise that cruelty starts
with a single thought.

Cruelty is not always measured
by the striking of another being.
Thoughts can be unkind.

People who have cruel thoughts
are capable of cruel actions.

If you are cruel to others,
you become a channel through which
The Dark Energies of The Life-Force
express themselves in the world.

The Dark Force
within The One
is slowly being conquered
by The Light of Love
within The All.

But Love will only succeed if
all creatures shun The Dark Side
and move over into The Light.

Be a Light-Giver,
and fill your thoughts and actions
with kindness and consideration.

To achieve a happier lifestyle
you must remove from your mind
any bitterness or malice that
you hold against others,
and resolve to love these souls
unconditionally
(which entails understanding
and forgiving their faults),
and in doing so you will place your feet
firmly on the road
towards greater contentment
and accelerated spiritual progression.

Spiritually developed beings
always resist the temptation to make
other souls suffer, because they know
that their uncharitable acts today
will return to be inflicted upon them
in the future, in full measure –
this is the operation of a Universal Law
which states that
each action will invoke
an equal reaction.

Send out thoughts of peace and goodwill
towards all Creation,
and be kind and merciful to those
who stand against you
and to those who defame your character,
for they are sorely in need of your love
and care.

Let your heart glow with magnanimity.

Be kind, also, to yourself.

And be realistic when trying to
achieve your targets –
you can only take one step at a time.

Celebrate your small victories,
one by one.

And keep on striving.

And realise that your deeds
will always speak much louder
than your words.

Remember that what you are doing now
will have a long-lasting effect
not only upon you
but also upon your fellow Pilgrims
along the Road.

Traveller on the Ancient Pathway:

Cleanse your mind,
your heart,
your soul —
and purify
your thoughts.

2.

Pay attention to
The Voice of your Soul…

And as the Traveller walked down the years
along the Way, admiring the perfect beauty of
the flowers that carpeted the Valley floor and
the magnificent world all around him, he
began to think about the beauty of his soul,
and about how he might develop its natural
spiritual powers, gifts and abilities, in order to
give something beautiful back to God. Then
quite suddenly, from near his solar-plexus, a
barely audible thought-voice cautioned him,
saying:

In order to tread safely
the ancient path of psychic awareness
and spiritual development,
initiates must possess great commitment,
great dedication, great trust; and above
all else — great love and patience.
They must also possess a strong-willed,
open, but questioning, mind,
and a bright intelligence
that is willing to learn
as much of the Truth as it can find...

While walking your spiritual pathway —
beware of unfolding your psychic
sensitivity at the cost of neglecting the
development of your spirituality.

And if your mind or emotions are
unbalanced — steer clear of unfolding your
psychic powers altogether; and, instead,
develop your spiritual nature,
your capacity to love —
for your soul's true level of
awareness and development
attracts to you both visible and invisible
intelligences who are in sympathy
with the real you,
and not with the image of the person
you believe yourself to be.

People who idolise psychic
and mediumistic abilities,
or the spirit guides, angelic inspirers,
and twin-souls
who co-operate with them,
misplace their reverence,
which then serves only to feed
the deluded part of themselves —
their egos.

Be grateful for your guidance,
but glorify only God,
your Almighty Mother and Father.

To develop sensitivity
you must first become more aware of
your own thoughts and feelings,
and then you must try to
empathise with others.

And here is a Key:
every soul is a part of
The Great Oversoul,
therefore soul-to-soul
telepathic links can be made.

And the fingerprints of the past
and the shadows of the future,
together with the ability
to see at a distance
and to travel instantaneously
to strange lands,
are all available to those souls
who can touch their Inner Senses.

Your Intuition,
Perception, and Sensitivity,
will heighten and increase
when you pay attention to them.

Practice makes perfect.

And if you can make the inside
as real to you as the outside is,
you will truly know
The Kingdom of Heaven,
and all that is in it.

The more sensitive your soul becomes,
the more it realises
that it must unfold itself on many levels:
mentally, spiritually,
emotionally, and physically.

Just keep on walking, thinking,
learning, questioning, serving,
expanding your mind
and developing your character,
and a degree of Self-realisation
will come —
for that is why you were born.

And as you struggle to deepen your
awareness, keep ever in mind that if you
wish to gain the guidance of
more advanced souls,
then you must advance your own
mental powers:
you must try to forge a common bond
with these more evolved beings
by emulating their greatness of
heart and mind.

Their friendship must be earned through
the expression of unconditional love
in all that you think, say and do.

And then they will guide you.

But do not expect your pathway
to be cleared for you completely.

Angels and friends will surely assist you
but the bulk of the clearing
must be done by you;
for if you learn
to see with the eyes of the spirit,
and not with the eyes of the body,
you will realise that you have played
a large part
in blocking your own progress.

And remember that the true mystical
experience is one in which the seeker
deepens his understanding of The Creator.

Never doubt the Omnipresence
of The Great Spirit,
within whom you originated,
for The Ever-Present Mind of God
sees Everything.

You, too, can see the unseen —
but only if you learn to perceive it
with your inner eyes.

Avert your gaze from the material world
and glimpse into spiritual light.

Can you see an answer?
If you can — act on it.

If you can't — wait patiently,
then look and listen again.

The answer will be given
only when the time is right.

Sensitivity is a wonderful blessing
but it can also be cumbersome curse.

Beware of your reputation
inflating your ego.

Fame and celebrity
are but fleeting shadows:
your motivation should be to serve,
and not to gain recognition
or reward for your efforts.

Spiritually aware people
seek God and render service to all,
and do not search for a spotlight
in which to dance.

Spiritually aware people
embrace The Silence.

The world is indeed a noisy
and materialistic place.

Try, therefore, to be more detached from
the noise and clamour of the world,
and from the brash emotions of others.

Remain tranquil within,
and you will touch the hidden power
that will help you to direct your life
successfully.

You can be a contemplative
in the heart of the world.

You are in the world,
but you do not need to be
of the world.

Detachment can be a jewel
in the crown of your life.

All those who care deeply
about the welfare of other souls
often need to detach themselves
from the horror of what they see.

Cultivate detachment,
and a small degree of indifference,
by all means – but detach with love:
and never lose your sense of duty,
responsibility, and care.

Detach yourself from loud noise,
which is a dissipating energy,
and rise above the turbulence of the world,
remembering always that silence
is filled with power.

*Seek out The Silence,
and embrace it lovingly.*

Incorporate a period of Absolute Silence
into your daily life.

To silence the mind and soul
is to experience the very
Essence of God's Spiritual Power
that dwells within you;
and once you truly touch
The Being of God,
you will gain perfect peace,
and have access to Everything.

To feel at peace and 'at-one'
with everything around you
and within you,
stop filling up your mind with
displacement activities,
with things to do.

Instead of constantly rushing around
the world being busy:
cease 'doing',
and start 'being'.

'Be' – don't 'do'.

Traveller,
you ask where is The Kingdom of Peace?

Search within your Self
and you will find it.

The Kingdom of Light,
where Peace and Power reign supreme,
is within you.

And once you have found
this Inner Realm of Tranquillity,
your eyes will look upon
the material world
in a completely different way.

When souls express love and peace,
powerful psychic rays spread outwards
from their hearts
and tremendous spiritual healing power
is generated.

Allow your peace to flow out of you,
and to radiate around you.

Blessed are the peace-makers.

Radiate your soul-light of peace,
and help to illuminate
the world's dark places,
which are many.

Bathe all angry hearts
in unconditional love.

Pray, and do good works;
and think kind thoughts.

In establishing an inner peace
and equilibrium
you will experience a much deeper sense of
contentment and satisfaction.

Try to walk the middle way:
not too much stress,
not too much relaxation.
Not too much food,
not too much fasting.

Think of others, but also think of yourself
and of your own needs —
do not neglect yourself.

And do not go to extremes
in your thinking, or in your feeling.

And whenever you feel threatened
or feel that you are in danger —
have perfect Trust.

Remain calm and peaceful,
and you will know what to do,
for The Spirit of Inspiration
will quietly instruct you.

But whatever will be,
will be.

Nevertheless,
rest assured that all the effort
you expend in developing your character
will earn you a prize
well worth the having –
a peace that passes all understanding,
and a freedom of the spirit that is granted
through a deeper awareness of God.

Meanwhile,
as you walk down the years on
a peaceful pathway
a firm commitment to non-violence
is one of the most spiritual gifts
that you could ever give back to
your Creator,
as a token of your gratitude to Him
for the very Gift of Life itself.

Then, quite out of the blue, a Voice of
Authority split the brilliant air asunder and
resounded in the depths of the Traveller's heart,
and spoke about the essence of his beliefs,
cautioning him, saying:

Keep ever in mind that your beliefs
run deeply through your soul,
colouring your actions and thoughts.

The Earthworld accommodates
a melting-pot of ideas:
you are all at different stages of evolution
and will never agree completely
with one another,
which is why you should
exercise tolerance in your dealings
with other creatures.

Believe this:
your soul knows why it has taken up
your body of flesh,
why it is visiting the Earth,
and what it must do while it is here.

Your soul created its own blueprint.

Commune with your soul
in the stillness of the night
and it will speak to you of its journey,
and it will tell you why it came.

If at first you do not hear
its still small voice – persevere;
for there is nothing hidden
which shall not be made known
to those who persist in their seeking.

Within your soul
resides The Energy of Creation
and the answer to every question,
just waiting to be discovered…

A wise soul sees his life
as a giant jigsaw puzzle
made up of thousands of
different experiences,
each one specifically designed to add
knowledge to his mind,
each challenge brought into being
to test the mettle of his spirit
and to build his character.

Day by day,
as the pattern
of your incarnation emerges,
insert what you believe to be
the correct piece into the picture,
then search for the next logical part.

And remember that as you live
and breathe, the soul within you
continuously records each of your thoughts
and deeds.

No one can 'get away' with anything;
the 'wrongs' that you have committed
will eventually have to be 'put right'
by you alone.

Always respect your soul,
and do not degrade it by uttering lies
and expressing violent thoughts.

Do not be cruel to other souls —
to people or to animals.

Respect their rights
and show them kindness.

All beings are your brethren;
and there, but for the grace of God,
go you.

All spiritual people find violence abhorrent
and they try to avoid it all costs;
but what can you do if dictators threaten
to impose their will on you,
or try to violate your human rights?

You have the right to make a stand.

You have the right
to defend your interests
and to protect your security.

But in order to resolve contentious issues,
you alone must decide
what direct action to take.

First, you must carefully plan
what you should to do,
then you must act swiftly on
your decision.

Take the initiative
and be decisive.

If you, yourself, have suffered from
violence or cruelty in childhood,
you must now break this circle of abuse.

Seek professional help for your difficulties,
and do everything in your power
to free yourself from the hurt and pain
caused by your past experiences.

Once you understand the causes of
your pain, you will be able to release
the hurt, and to finally break
a malicious circle of wrong-doing —
and the children of tomorrow
will thank you for it.

We are all children at heart,
in need of love and appreciation.

The children of today
are the citizens of tomorrow,
so give them a good start in life.

Teach them about the importance
of loving and caring for other souls,
and of protecting their environment.

Instil in them
a sense of personal responsibility
that will help them
to respect others' rights and property.

Teach them to be kind to animals.

Help them to understand
what you understand:
the importance of sharing and of listening,
and also of freely giving.

Remember that although
The Children of God have advanced
technologically and scientifically,
spiritually their souls still limp along,
preferring to glory in the past
rather than to make dynamic changes
which will propel them towards
a brighter, much healthier future.

Do not be afraid to implement
radical new changes
all around you in your own life.

If you wish to progress spiritually:
first examine your level of tolerance,
and then increase it.

Spiritual progression comes
when you expand your awareness,
when you cease to think only of yourself
and begin to consider the rights of others.

How well do you know yourself?

Here are two spiritual keys
for you to think about,
and against which you may measure
the current state of your soul's evolution:

Those who would be cruel to an animal,
would be cruel to a human being.

Those who fully understand and
appreciate what is 'good',
can only do so because they are acquainted
with its opposite force.

What kind of soul are you?

Find it in your heart
to think of all those beings who feel lost,
unloved and uncared for,
of all those beleaguered spirits
who are starving in the streets,
and of a myriad others who are daily used
and abused across the planet.

Pray for those souls
who are less fortunate than you are,
then stride out purposefully
into the world
and do something positive to help them.

There are many 'unlucky' and troubled
minds who need your help.

As a being who recognises
its eternal nature,
what kind of example are
you setting for other souls to see?

The young always look to their elders
for guidance, hoping to find
an ideal pattern to emulate and follow.

But if your life is poor in spirit
and bereft of kind deeds,
your followers will never reach
their full potential.

And if your deeds are half-hearted
and ineffective, your followers
will not be likely to succeed.

And if your spiritual words are stamped
with ignorance, you will fail to move
the minds of those who follow you,
and to make them think and grow.

Once in a while, Voyager,
take an objective look at your own mind,
and particularly at what you believe in.

Always exercise caution
when following any set of beliefs,
for if you believe in something
one hundred per cent
this could be unhealthy
because your mind is then closed
to any new possibilities.

Whatever your belief-system is,
if it makes you a better person,
then it is right for you.

If your beliefs teach you to be loving
and tolerant,
then they are a good set of instructions.

You should test the validity of your beliefs
at the bar of your intelligence.

Lazy minds
belong to humanity's followers;
intelligent minds
belong to humanity's leaders and thinkers.

Accelerate your spiritual growth:
do not be a follower — be a thinker.

You have the right
to voice your beliefs and opinions freely,
and to live your life
in the way you see fit,
provided that your thoughts and actions
do not provoke violence in others
or threaten their peace,
stability,
or wellbeing.

And as you walk along the Road:
always be grateful and polite.
It will cost you very little energy to say
"Please", "Thank you",
or "I'm sorry."

It is often easy to recognise
the spiritual ignorance in other people –
but take time to cleanse your own mind
of any ignorance.

Ignorance births superstition.

Do not embrace ignorance
and make it your own –
educate yourself.

Banish the darkness of superstition
from your life,
and embrace the light of knowledge.

And do not believe
in a mythical creature called 'the devil',
for there is no such being.

If man wants to see a well of havoc
and unkindness —
he can look in the mirror.

The Darker Side of The Life-Force
is inherent in all beings — each one of us
is capable of hard-heartedness
and wickedness.

It is man, himself,
who uses The Life-Force
for misguided or 'evil' purposes.

Do not blame a fantasy
for what has happened to you
or to those whom you love.

"What, then, is The Truth?" cried out the anxious Traveller, emerging from some shaded woodland back out into the brilliant sunshine flooding the Valley floor.

"If you Angels who speak to me do so because you love me – then give me some kind of sign! Show me a path to follow! And speak to me of Truth, and of Judgement!" he called again.

And suddenly a deep but steady voice stirred his conscience and said:

No one can possess
the whole of The Truth;
you may each have a small portion of it,
but no one knows the entirety of
Absolute Truth.

You must be patient.

Look much deeper –
and listen carefully for the truth
that is hidden behind the words
that you read or hear.

Take note of what is happening
around you
and within you.

But do not simply see
what the eyes see,
and do not simply hear
what the ears hear.

Spiritual people are not afraid to speak
the truth as they see it
or to express their feelings,
but they try not to cause
unnecessary distress.

Everyone benefits from hearing the truth
because then they know
exactly where they stand.

But wise tongues are often silent.

The success of your relationships
depends on your thoughts and feelings
being honestly shared,
and on being truthfully –
but not hurtfully –
expressed.

Speak honestly at all times.

Do not allow falsehood to take root
in your mind,
for it grows like a virulent weed –
and, instead of a small seed of deceit,
you will soon have a mighty tree of lies
growing within you.

Remember that whenever you
deceive others, you are, in fact,
deceiving yourself.

Seekers after Truth
must possess great hearts
filled with unconditional love
for all of God's creatures,
for only then will they be able to
attract to themselves the greatest spiritual
guidance, which emanates from
highly-evolved souls who are
living in Realms of Purity and Light.

Pilgrim along the Way:
open up your mind
to The Truth.

Truth builds her nest
only in the branches of
an open mind;
and as a gift to those who love her
she will set their spirits free.

Do not forget that
The Creator and His Angels
know the person you truly are,
for they can see
your true state of soul-evolution
clearly displayed in the golden bowl of
energy about your head,
and in the auric fields of sensitivity
generated within your mind.

Those who assume an air of
false goodness are hypocrites
because while thinking one thought
they speak another.

But those who express the truth
are being honest with themselves
and with others.

Which of these two descriptions
applies to you?

Keep in mind that
God has charged all Servants of the Spirit
with the responsibility of sharing
with others the spiritual truths that
they have found,
for Knowledge is Power,
and Knowledge empowers its possessor.

Hold up your torch of spiritual knowledge
in this dark world,
for it was given to you
first to liberate your own mind,
and then to free the minds of others.

The Earth is teeming with beings
who are struggling through life
held back by the curse of ignorance,
but their souls are longing for truth
and peace.

You should not neglect your duty
to do whatever you can to release
mankind,
and the animal kingdom,
from mental, emotional, spiritual,
and physical pain.

And now we speak of Judgement:
in the Hereafter
there is no celestial judgement day;
there is no angelic jury which will
condemn or praise you.

Your soul is the judge and the jury —
right here, right now;
and in the future.

Exercise your judgement wisely.

Do not be hasty;
and try always to be kind to yourself
and to others.
Treat others compassionately,
as you yourself would like to be treated.

And do not condemn
your fellow Travellers:
you do not have the insight to see
their fate.

Neither can you fully appreciate
the circumstances which have made them
take the actions they have taken.

Do not condemn – try to understand.

Speak together,
and you will quickly realise that
your previous judgements may well have
been tainted with prejudice,
or they may have been flawed.

But do not be afraid of judgement.

Criticism, whether it is negative
or positive, will help you to
grow as a personality
if you can look at it objectively,
to discover if there is any truth in it.

If truth is present,
you can then work towards
correcting your behaviour.

If you judge that you have 'wronged'
another soul in this life,
or in a previous one,
you will have to repay your debt
by making amends through service
and acts of kindness.

No one can cheat this Law.

You are continuously developing your
character by facing and overcoming
the multifarious challenges and conflicts
of the heart and mind that you have
attracted to yourself through
the Law of Karma,
which is the Law of Cause and Effect.

However,
do not judge your actions too severely.

Each decision you made in the past
seemed right to you at the time
when you made it.

Everyone would make alterations
to their life-plan
if they were given half the chance.

But what is gone is gone —
and you cannot change it.

Everyone makes mistakes.

You can, however, be sensible
and learn from your past errors
of judgement;
but in so doing
do not weigh yourself down
with unnecessary guilt or regret.

But know this:
The Law of Personal Responsibility
ensures that you alone
will carry the burden of your mistakes,
and that you alone must rectify them.

No one can remove from your shoulders
the acts that you have committed —
only you can do this.

This Law cannot be abrogated.

You are responsible for what you do.

And the Traveller looked up into the vaulted heavens and cried out from the centre of his being, "Great God: I am listening! Although I'm in my adult years, yet am I still weak and uneducated; but you are Mighty and All-Powerful! I've tried to understand your Laws – but please help me in my seeking!

"How should I live, Great Spirit, in order to be happy, healthy and contented?"

And the skies parted and the sun went out.

And the Traveller lifted up his face to the heavens – and set against the backdrop of Infinity he saw a vast panoply of shimmering stars, a host of Ancient Watchers who have kept guard over mankind for untold centuries.

And from the depths of inner space the calm voice of an Ambassador of God addressed him, saying:

If all The Laws of God
were to be recorded,
the world would be filled with books.

Live your life according to The Laws of
The Great Spirit and you will attain
harmony, happiness and contentment,
health and ease.
But if you do not align yourself with
these Laws then disharmony,
misery and discontent, ill-health and
disease will be your reward.

When conditions around you are difficult,
discover which Laws you have broken,
then realign your thinking:
reset your pathway;
reassess your conduct –
then stride into a new day
with a more positive mind
and a more purposeful step.

Everything in the Universe
is in a state of perfect balance:
negativity balances positivity;
'good' balances 'evil'; love balances hate –
all these forces are in perfect equilibrium.
If this were not so, the Universe
would cease to be held together.
There are two sides to each situation;
if you examine the positive
and the negative,
the 'rights' and the 'wrongs' of
all circumstances and conditions,
you will gain a much better
understanding of why certain events are
happening.

The Universal Laws rule Supreme,
and no one can escape the consequences
of his thoughts.

Those who break The Law
will pay the price.

Everything that you have ever done
has been projected into the Universe
as energy-vibrations.
Throughout your life
you have put into operation
countless Causes,
and these Causes do not 'die' —
they will return to you
with their precise Effects.

Effect follows Cause
with mathematical precision.

You will reap what you have sown,
and you cannot escape the harvest —
for this is part of the Plan.

In the Divine Masterplan,
which is continuously operating in,
and influencing, every life,
events will occur
only at their appointed times.

Why, then do you worry about
the future?

Live for today.
Rejoice in this moment.

The future will take care of itself.

Your future will soon come to meet you:
it is approaching minute by minute.

Only God knows
what will greet you today,
and He will grant you the strength
and the courage
to conquer the challenges
that lay before you.

Each event in your life has been carefully
planned to challenge your spirit,
to build your character,
and to expand and enlighten your mind.

Face your life with courage and
with a determination to succeed,
for behind all of Life's trials
there is a Mighty Power
pressing through each thought and action:
it is The Great Designer,
which is evolving Itself
through personally sharing
in your experiences.

It is no accident that you are living
on Earth
in these circumstances.

Know that there is no such thing as
an accident or a co-incidence:
everything is brought about by
The Natural Laws
in operation.

You are playing your part
in a Masterplan.

You find yourself where you are, because
that is where you are supposed to be
at this time.

Soldier on.

Acknowledge that
God is The Supreme Governor.

Politicians, monarchs,
tyrants, despots, guardians,
and others who consider it their duty
or privilege to rule over men
spend only a short time on the Earth;
their power is temporal —
it will soon pass away.

But The Great Spirit will stand for ever.

Try to understand
your Creator's Laws
because they are continuously pressing
through every aspect of your life,
every second of every minute,
of every hour,
of every day.

Discover the Causes
of each happening
and you will obtain the Keys
that will open or lock
every door in your life.

Know that there is no such thing
as chance — all is ruled by Law.

This is not easy to perceive,
nor is it often a palatable thought,
but nevertheless it is the truth.

There are Spiritual Plans,
and plans within plans,
outworking themselves all of the time;
some of their workings
may be obvious to you,
but many of them will remain unseen
and unfelt
until you meet their effects head-on.

The laws of man are flawed,
because man is flawed,
but the Laws of God are Perfect.

Because the Natural Laws
were created
and are administered by
Perfect Justice
it has been ordained that each soul
will receive only what it has earned,
irrespective of how it may feel about this.

But happy is the man who recognises
that all things are passing,
and that nothing remains
in a constant state.

Life is all about movement,
change, and progression.

Stride forward confidently.

Everything is in a state of continual
change: you, your loved ones, your life,
your thoughts – everything.

The Universe is forever evolving
and expanding – nothing stands still.

Because of this Law
you must learn to 'go with the flow';
you must accept change as a part of life.

You cannot hold on to the past:
you must flow with the present
and drift towards the future.

To stand still is impossible.
To go back is impossible.

Like the willow tree you must learn
to bend and sway
under the weight of the breeze.

Realise that everything in the Universe
is interconnected.

The whole fabric of life
is intricately woven,
and you are an important thread
in its weft and weave.

You cannot exist without
a myriad other energies and beings –
so join in with The March of Life,
and do not delude yourself into thinking
that you are any more 'special'
than anyone else.

You are not an island to be set apart
from the world,
with no connections to other souls.

Every thing, and every one,
is interdependent.
We are all in this together.

Do not isolate yourself from society,
or from contact with other beings.

Do not be self-centred:
others may stand in need of your wisdom,
your presence, or your help.

All is One, and One is All;
and because of this,
help and personal guidance are always
available to you —
all you have to do is ask for them.

No one promised you that life on Earth
would be easy,
yet the pathway must be walked.

At times of stress
it is important to ask yourself
this question:
"Why has this happened to me?"

And you will find that the answer is:
for reasons of soul-growth,
so that you may advance your
personal evolution.

Sometimes people can be callous
and life can seem too hard a struggle,
but you must bear up bravely and patiently
in the knowledge that the darkness of
a gathering storm cannot last for ever.

Soon the black clouds will disperse
and the downpour will end;
and when the skies have emptied,
a rainbow will appear.

This is God's promise
to all of His Children.

Just do your best.
No one in this world or in the next
can ask any more of you.

Apply yourself diligently to your work:
concentrate and be attentive.

Do not give only half the effort
you know you are capable of giving.

Do not short-change others, and you,
in turn, will not be short-changed
by your Father,
who sees All.

Seeker:
when you retire to bed,
can you think these thoughts?:

"Today I did my best in all that I did.
I gave service
to the best of my ability."

If you can think this,
and it is true,
then your reward will be great.

There are bound to be times
when you feel dissatisfied.

At such times:
change the circumstances of your life
which you can change,
and accept with grace the conditions life
that you cannot change.

No one is a puppet who must dance
to the strings you pull –
their souls are as free as yours is:
they have freewill, just as you do,
but it is limited by the all-encompassing
Natural Laws.

Traveller:
there will be times in your life
when you will have to cultivate
the grace of acceptance.

But remember that you are never alone:
surrounding you in the invisible worlds
there is a multitude of souls,
watching, guarding,
guiding, advising,
and inspiring you.

Physically, you may be
the only person in the room,
but spiritually all of the space around you
is filled with many minds living
at different levels of spiritual, moral,
and soul attainment.

They will inspire you,
should you desire it.

But be mindful of The Law of
Like Attracts Like:
you will draw to you the attention
of those who are existing
in the same planes of thought as yourself.

Remember that you will receive
what you deserve – no more, and no less.

If you want happiness –
make others happy.

If you want love – love others.

If you need a friend – be a friend.

Whatever you project into
The Stream of Consciousness
will eventually return to you,
in full measure.

And always act wisely,
for whatever one soul takes from another,
will eventually be taken away
from the taker.

What is important to you?

Whatever is important to you,
give this to others
so that it may eventually be given to you.

If you plant a rose,
only a rose will grow.

If you shine forth Love,
only Love will return to you;
and this same Law applies if you radiate
to others the negative energies of hatred,
anger, intolerance, selfishness,
self-pity and self-indulgence.

Traveller:
be careful what you wish for.

And if you feel unloved and neglected,
or that you are being treated unkindly,
this is because somewhere in the past
you have not loved others,
not respected their rights
or treated them with kindness,
and this includes your treatment of
the souls in the animal kingdom.

You are now experiencing Divine Justice
in action:
this spiritual sequence of exact Effects
following their precise Causes
will now play itself out –
and it cannot be broken.

So do not waste your time
hammering on doors that remain
continually closed to you.

Carefully review your situation
with clean eyes,
and look for an open gateway nearby,
or a new window through which
you may pass without obstruction.

Each happening in your life,
whether pleasant or otherwise,
is filled with hidden purpose.

It is easy to welcome joy and gladness,
and not so easy to welcome
pain and unhappiness,
but the effects must be borne
with a brave and courageous heart.

Once every debt has been paid,
your difficulties will ease.

But beware!

You are still transmitting Causes,
and you will receive their Effects
in the future.

And all down the years
throughout your journey,
pay heed to The Law of Co-operation.

Do not dominate –
work always in partnerships that respect
everyone's rights, and their privacy.

And let the decisive one who leads
be as humble as the one who follows.

3.

The Voice of your Spirit is Speaking to you…

The Traveller was now passing through his middle years, through that time of life when the emotions are calmer and the personality becomes more placid. He moved steadily along the Valley floor towards a wooded area, and when a thick canopy of leaves above him shaded out the Sun he felt fearful and alone, because he was in semi-darkness. But suddenly a shaft of Golden Light parted the canopy and fixed him in its radiance, and a composed voice vibrated within the energy-ray and said:

Traveller, remember your spirit.
Do not neglect to feed it
with silence, breath, and power.

Energise it with The Cosmic Rays of
Life — breathe them in
through the top of your head
and through your solar plexus,
as if they were air.

Remember: your soul needs to be fed.

Man's spirit receives the least of
his attentions because it thrives on
the expressing of Love.

You ask how you can develop your spirit?

You have to give, in order to receive.

As you outpour your Love in service
to others, you will automatically draw
back into your own spirit
more of God's Beneficent Life-Power.

You have to serve, in order to nurture
and unfold the power of your spirit.

Know that invisible spiritual and
physical energies are constantly feeding
your soul, your body, and your mind.

Simply by walking through the world
and interacting with others,
you are feeding and energising
your psychic Self.

Move through the world, then,
and play your part in it.

Do not lock yourself away to wither and
collapse for want of the life-giving
energies of love and kindness
which are yours by birthright,
which are yours for the giving
and for the taking.

There are three qualities that all spiritual
souls must possess before they can set out
on a successful road of serving God
and mankind:
Dedication, Commitment,
and a deep-seated sense of Responsibility.
You must dedicate yourself to your
spiritual work completely – there must be
no half measures.
You must be totally committed to
fulfilling your spiritual duties –
come what may.
Without question, you must accept
personal responsibility for your actions,
and behave responsibly. You must be a
reliable person and keep your promises
and never let The World of Spirit down.

If you do not possess these qualities:
rethink your mission,
for your spiritual work will not be as
fruitful as it ought to be.

And do not forget that
The Spirit within you
is The Spirit of the Breeze,
and The Soul of the Sky;
in Essence,
we are all the same…

And when the Traveller stopped to rest his tired body by sitting on a hillock, he commented to anyone who was listening, "Voices of the Angel World! I have walked far, learned a great deal, and suffered much on my journey. When the day comes for me to pass from this vale of anguish and to move into Infinity, will I be rewarded for the service I have given to mankind? Surely I have finished my work now, and am worthy to progress into The Light?"

And out of a Radiant Cloud high above him in the azure sky, an androgynous ethereal voice addressed him, saying:

The time is not yet.

And no worthwhile spiritual progression can come to you,
until you learn to be completely honest with yourself.

You cannot claim to be
a spiritual personality
unless you serve others compassionately
to the bitter end,
without thought of any reward
or personal gain.

Your actions always will
identify what is in your soul.

The label on the outside of a parcel
does not always identify what is inside it.

On Earth,
your appearance and demeanour
can mislead the multitudes —
but you cannot fool God or His Angels,
to whom you are completely
and utterly known.

Unto your Self be true.

Remember that Work and Service
bring dignity and purpose to your life.

Work is worship.

Selflessness and self-abnegation
are high spiritual ideals
that are not easy to attain.

Think on these things.

Your direction is governed not so much
by the forces that surround you
but by the forces that pulse within you,
and which are now influencing
every facet of your being.

The coin of the soul is service —
do not be spiritually bankrupt.

Of what value is it to be materially
wealthy if your soul is pitifully lacking
in humanity, warmth and love?

One day you will have to leave your
wealth behind you on the Earth,
but you will take your soul with you
into Eternity.

Store up for yourself treasures
in The Everlasting Kingdom.

But while you are here on this planet,
serve others with a happy heart
and you will build up within yourself
a tide of happiness and fulfilment that will
wash away
all thoughts of loneliness,
and will bring a sense of purpose
to your days.

Those souls who are numbered
among the great and the good
have given generously of their time
and energy to help the world.

They have sacrificed
much of their free time
and expended much of their free energy
in order to help their ailing brethren.

Will you do likewise?

But if your duties are characterised
by a cavalier, unsympathetic,
and ill-mannered attitude
you are setting yourself up as a dictator —
and all dictators, without exception,
will fall.

It is only by your example that you teach.

Traveller,
what kind of role-model are you?

It is true that if you align yourself with
Love and Service
you will be tested to the uttermost.

You will need great discipline, patience,
kindness and restraint,
and a forgiving nature
in order to succeed.

To be a disciple, you must have discipline:
you will need to resist impatience
and impulsiveness.

You will have to sacrifice many pleasures
in order to serve –
but your reward in Heaven will be great.

Although your work and service
are important,
remember that no one is irreplaceable.

Delegate some of your workload to others.

Trust others a little more,
and grant them the opportunity to serve.

And in your busy world – prioritise.

Take an unemotional look at your tasks
and responsibilities, and deal with the
most important jobs first.

The less important tasks
can wait a while.

As soon as you fulfil one duty
another will rise to take its place,
for life is all about work and service
and about the expending of your time,
thought and energy.

You will never retire from the work
you were born to do.

Both in your workplace
and in your daily life,
your spiritual principles play a vital
part in maintaining your emotional
and mental health.

Do not be lured by worldly temptations
into overruling your principles.

Stick to your principles,
for they are worth far more
than a fleeting moment of glory
or self-gratification.

And try to be tolerant of others.

Tolerance is one of the hallmarks of
a spiritual personality;
and another is the expression of
unconditional love.

You must also learn to tolerate your own
shortcomings; and in order to aid your
spiritual progress: periodically, make an
honest and careful appraisal of your
character, your thoughts and actions —
a process that should be undertaken in
a calm and objective way.

In recognising your shortcomings,
you may find the way to correct them.

Acknowledge that it is healthy for you
to have a sense of self-tolerance
and a good dose of self-esteem.

You are a unique being:
there never has been,
and there never will be,
another person like you in this world.

Do not allow yourself or others
to lower your sense of self-value.

Respect yourself a little more.

You have developed your mind
through many lifetimes of hard work,
and you have earned the right
to recognise your own worth.

There is nothing wrong with being
proud of your achievements.

You have a problem only when your pride
inflates your ego or gives you a puffed-up
sense of self-importance,
which may generate within you
arrogance and self-righteousness.

Temper your pride with humility
and you will be much a healthier
and more spiritually developed person,
and many more people will befriend you.

4.

Pay Heed to
The Voice of Love...

And now that the Traveller was in his settled years, in the time when his hair had greyed and his actions were less hurried, his mind had become more open to new thoughts, and his heart had become softened by the many trials he had encountered during his pilgrimage through life.

As he approached the last quarter of the Valley of Wisdom, he stopped and glanced back along the road he had travelled.

Then he looked forward, and wondered if he should try to climb the greatest mountain of all.

But he decided that the climb would be too perilous and too difficult for him.

Or would it be?

Then he wondered, "What is the most important lesson that I have learned?"

And within The Light of his Heart a highly evolved soul spoke, saying:

**Without Love,
we are nothing.**

Remember
The Great Commandment
taught by the prophets
and spiritual masters of old,
and of which the Nazarene
reminded the world, when he said:

"Love one another,
as I have loved you."

Speak of love.

Act in the spirit of love.

Be a light of love,
and shine your light into the darkness of
hatred and misunderstanding.

You are an Ambassador for
The Great Spirit, therefore act accordingly,
in a spirit of compassion.

Fill your thoughts and words with love;
be patient with others, and treat them
with respect and consideration.

Remember that no one is perfect.
No one perfect has ever been born
on the Earth.

Always champion the cause of love.

Enthrone love in your own heart
and let its compassionate rays
illuminate the world within you,
and everyone around you will benefit from
its healing radiance.

Deliver this healing power of love to
anyone, anywhere in the Universe,
simply by focusing your mind on
its transmission –
distance is no obstacle.

Give encouragement to each loving act
and thought.

Love is the most powerful force
in the Universe.

Love has many forms.

Consensual sexual love is an expression of
thoughts and emotions;
and it is good that you should celebrate
your feelings for one another.

Spiritual Love can never be wrong,
and those who think that it is
are narrow-minded
and unseeing.

Avoid pettiness of thought.

Whenever you decide to express
the mighty power of Unconditional Love,
people are cleansed and transformed by it.

Let love guide you.

Choose to heal,
and not to inflict pain or suffering.

Decide to create peace,
and not to destroy harmony.

The choice is yours:
but remember that it is the spiritual duty
of the higher forms of intelligence
to take care of the lower forms,
and not to exploit them.

Try to be more compassionate
and generous.

It is the little acts of kindness
that make life worth living,
and all this starts with you.

A daily act of kindness from you
will act like a small wave:
spreading outwards
it will join other waves, which will
generate mighty tides of compassion
that will eventually circle
the face of the Earth.

You can make a difference.

Remember that everyone wants to feel
accepted and to be appreciated,
and you can effect great spiritual changes
in people if they know that you are
grateful for their efforts.

When you treat others with kindness,
spiritually the whole world benefits
because your healing thought-energies are
then passed on from soul to soul,
gathering momentum as they go.

Always look upon others
with compassionate eyes —
but develop a willpower of steel
to complement your gentle heart.

Your mind must be strong,
but your heart should be benevolent.

And at least once a day be grateful for
what has been given to you.

Be grateful for the love and respect
radiated towards you from your friends
and family, from the beings who reside
within the worlds of soul,
and from other unexpected
and hidden sources.

There is so much to be grateful for —
in your material circumstances,
in your mind, body and soul.

Unhappy are those who constantly
complain about the things
they perceive as being 'wrong'
in their lives.

The Law of Attraction pulls towards
them the very misery that they fear.

If you want to be happy –
change your attitude.

It is said that
when a Pilgrim on a dusty road
stopped a Holy Man and begged of him,
"Wise One, I am leaving that miserable
town behind me and moving on to a new
life in the next city. Tell me:
will I be happy there?"

The Holy Man asked,
"Were you happy in the town
that you just left?"

"No, I was miserable there."

"Then you will be miserable in your new
city," said the Guru.

For the next few days, as often as you can,
vocally thank God for the millions of
blessings He freely bestows upon you:
for your ability to think,
for your health,
your comfortable bed, your home,
your shoes, for the food you eat,
for your friends,
and even for the air that you breathe.

Unhappiness will soon disperse
and you will begin drawing towards you
the very joy that you desire.

And as you walk among the world,
as far as possible
adopt the principle of harmlessness
towards all living things.

Harmlessness
is an expression of unconditional love.

Resolve never again to harm another
being, which includes those souls
in the animal kingdom.

From today onwards stop eating meat
and generate within you a greater respect
for The Spirit of God which resides
within your sentient brethren
in the animal kingdom,
who are still so cruelly abused
by the spiritually ignorant.

In order to spiritually progress,
you must change:
you must increase your ability
to be compassionate, and you must respect
the planet upon which you live.

Does your love reach out beyond the scope
of yourself, and of your immediate family?
Here is one way to check if it does:

Are you kind to animals?
Don't eat meat —
don't buy it or cook it for anyone else.

Do you think God's Angels are pleased
when a callous being terminates a life?

You cannot create Life,
therefore you have no right to take it.

Be kind to other souls.

Resolve to respect one another,
and also to show compassion to the souls
in the animal kingdom.

Do not purchase cosmetics or household
goods that have been tested on animals.

Traveller:
be more considerate.

Pilgrim on the Road,
the choice is yours:

You can either love or hate;
you can either harm or care;
you can either kill or cure.

But whichever way you choose:
you will be held personally accountable
for your actions
by The One who Sees All.

The way to develop spiritually is to care.

Care for others,
and also for yourself.

The Healing Power of Divine Love
can care for others through you,
and It can cure all pain.

And remember on your journey that
the world is your country
and its people are your family.

Voyager,
every living thing is related to you:
all conscious creatures are your brothers
and sisters; they are your fellow Travellers
along the Way.

Therefore, honour them,
and respect them.

You are all friends sharing a small planet;
and the value of friendship is enormous.

Never undervalue your friendships —
nurture them and allow them to grow
and mature, because souls need the
energies of other souls around them.

Your friends are your safe harbour
in a storm; they are your comfort
in your hour of distress —
cherish them,
and never take them for granted.

And be a true friend to yourself:
treat yourself with love and respect,
as you would treat a treasured companion.

Above all:
love and respect one another,
and serve each other
with a willing heart,
remembering always that
true love serves for its own sake.

Because you are surrounded by
Hosts of Invisible Angels,
you should never feel lonely,
neglected or unloved.

If your life seems empty —
just look around you again,
and you will find that God has filled it
with many dear souls who love you.

And in all your dealings with others:
listen to the voice of your conscience.

Within you there is a Divine Monitor,
which is your governor.

You know when you have done
something wrong
or done something right.

You know when you have harmed
another soul.

But remember that when you hurt other
people, you are also hurting yourself.

People are not pleased when others treat
them with callous disdain.

Therefore do not be callous,
unsympathetic or apathetic –
be caring.

Try to be forgiving, and give all of your
relationships a second chance.

Trust people again, and do not condemn
them because of their past records.

The saying
'I can forgive, but I can't forget'
is a truism,
for all of your thoughts are indelibly
recorded deep within the chasms of
your mind, and they can never be lost
or erased.

But we have all made mistakes —
we are all fallible beings,
and as such we all crave opportunities
to set the record straight.

May you find it in your heart
to forgive and to heal,
to make amends
and to set yourself in concord with
those you think may have wronged you
in the past.

If you forgive those who have hurt you,
used you or despised you,
you will express in your world
a positive Spirit of Love,
and it is better to do this than to add to
the world's alarming negative energy-store
of anger, spite and hatred.

Spurn anger.

Curb your temper.

Banish hatred from your being;
and never be spiteful.

Peace will reign on Earth
only when human beings learn to Love –
and Peace starts within you.

The fuel that fires up Peace and Hope in
the human breast
is Loving Thoughts and Deeds.

You must be the one to heal, to forgive,
to nurture and to care;
you must be the one
to settle disagreements.

*Surely, now is the time to
forgive, and to lay to rest
any misunderstandings and grievances
you may hold against those whom
you ought to love and serve?*

Without exception,
we have all made mistakes.

Remember that to err is human
but to forgive is Divine.

Correct your wrong-doings now,
and create a brighter future for yourself
and others.

Traveller,
now that you have an understanding of
God, and of the way in which
His Power works,
you can turn your attention
to your *Self*.

You are full of passions and desires.

Examine your motives carefully,
and see the world with straight
and clear vision:
do not look at yourself or others through
rose-coloured spectacles,
but try to see people as they truly are.

No one is perfect; not one of us.

It is our human frailties that make us
attractive and mark us out
as individuals.

Some simple self-analysis
is a healthy undertaking.

As you stride into emotional maturity,
find out why you behave
in the way that you do.

People who believe that great age brings
wisdom are not always correct:
the young can be wise, because wisdom
springs from an awareness of God's Laws
and from a willingness to change
and to progress the Self.

Keep everything simple and you will
understand The Mysteries of Life,
which are often hidden from the wise.

Fortunate is the man who fully
understands the motivation
behind his ambitions.

Ambition is a powerful force which,
if misdirected, can create havoc with your
soul's state of equilibrium,
rhythm and health.

Nurture your ambitions, by all means,
but temper them wisely;
and, most importantly –
realise why they were born.

And do not bottle-up your feelings
to the point where you make yourself
emotionally ill or deeply distressed.

Remember that your emotions
are very real energies
which need to be expressed.

Express your feelings.

Voice your opinions and thoughts,
and you will feel much better afterwards.

And whenever you feel anxious:
be still;
take a cool, fresh look at your life,
at yourself, and at others,
and then try again to understand
your circumstances.

Anxiety occurs when a soul doesn't know
whether to fight or run,
when it doesn't know whether
to fulfil its duties or
to indulge in its desires.

Travel the middle pathway
and let your worries go.

Fulfil your responsibilities
but also taste the joys of pleasure and fun.

To control your passions and desires
and to spiritually progress
you must make an effort each day
to be more mindful of,
and be more considerate towards,
all souls,
everywhere.

Try to be more empathetic;
try to be more thoughtful.

Seeker,
never forget that you are a Child of God,
and therefore everything that you do
is important.

But you cannot hope to rebuild your life
unless you make space upon which to lay
new foundations:
sometimes destruction must come
before regeneration can begin.

But do not destroy institutions or
relationships, unless they become corrupt.

The power to destroy and then to rebuild
should always be used wisely.

And try to avoid conflict:
pursue a peaceful way —
a way of reconciliation,
a way of consideration,
rather than a way filled with arguments
and disagreements, which bring more
pain and anger into the world.

But if the peaceful way fails
and conflict seems inevitable:
be as gentle as you can be,
as understanding as you can be,
and use the minimum possible force
behind your words and deeds.

Do not add to the vast swirling sea of
anger and hatred
that is already in the world.

You must learn the art of compromise;
you must learn to give and take in all
your dealings with others.

Recognise that you cannot ever have it all
your own way – this is impossible.

Do not try to impose your will on others
and imagine that they will always do
your bidding, willingly or otherwise;
this desire stems from
a false sense of your own
self-importance.

The Way to happiness is paved with
Co-operation and Collaboration.

Whenever you disagree with others
try to settle your disputes amicably and
reasonably, and in good spirit,
showing respect for one
another's feelings and opinions.

But if this action does not resolve
contentious issues:
you have the right to defend yourself.

You have the right to protect your human
rights and to secure your interests,
your health and your wellbeing.

People who say, "There is no anger in me,"
are living in a fantasy realm.

Anger springs from the basic instinct of
Fear, which is a part of everyone's psyche.

To progress spiritually
you must acknowledge and accept
the darker sides of your personality
as well as the lighter aspects of it.

Progress comes to all those who learn
to control their minds and emotions.

Bitterness and anger
are dark siblings.

Bitterness eats away at your state of
health and erodes your peace of mind.

Bitterness makes you bigoted
and small-minded, hurtful,
and deeply unattractive to others.

Bitterness is a form of revenge that may
transmute into violence or wrong-action
if left unguarded.

Do not be malicious, or quarrelsome.

Use your anger positively:
anger can motivate you to serve.

You can express anger via destruction,
disruption and degradation – or you can
channel it more positively into fighting
injustice and inequality, into combating
the many ills that plague the
people of the Earth.

Screaming can release
anger-tensions that have built up
within your mind –
but do not make a habit of it:
a short, powerful shout can be beneficial,
but prolonged screaming can damage
your mind and unbalance your psyche.

Acknowledge that aggression is
the reverse side of the coin of love –
and that these two aspects coexist,
side by side, in everyone.

Realise this and you can transform your
aggression, and your desire to dominate,
into energetic forces that can be
skilfully redirected
into more fruitful projects.

And expel fear from your mind.

Fear is a bad counsellor —
it negates, and brings in its train a great
deal of nullifying and harmful
psychic power.

Do not be afraid -- be confident
and courageous.

Never allow fear to
paralyse your important actions.

Do not fear what tomorrow may bring,
for your worries may never materialise.

Neither should you stress yourself with
the details of long-term plans and ideas,
for they may never come to fruition.

Concern yourself only with solving
your short-term problems,
as and when they arrive.

And do not be a materialist.

Try to be generous with your property —
and do not steal another's possessions.

Covetousness can create intense pain.

The passions of envy and jealousy
often compel a person to want to possess
something that may not belong to him.

Keep these traits well under control,
and do not let them control you.

Banish greed and possessiveness from your
life and you will set yourself on the road
towards attaining emotional stability.

Recognise that greed and possessiveness
are troublesome bedmates,
then peer closely into your heart —
and cast out these powerful,
negative forces.

Soul upon the Road:
always avoid pessimism.

Pessimism is an unhealthy state.

Optimism is a healthier state.

But Realism is by far the best state in
which to achieve good mental health
and emotional equilibrium.

And always be discreet and use tact
in your dealings with other souls,
and do not embarrass them.

Tact and discretion are the hallmarks of
a spiritual person who is sensitive
to the needs of others.

Remember to keep others' confidences,
for everyone has the right to some privacy.

And make beauty your watchword:
beauty of speech and thought;
beauty of movement and deed.

Speak kindly to all souls,
and avoid vulgarity.

The temple of your body
and the capacity of your mind are like
beautiful instruments that should be
played upon by your soul
with grace and dignity.

And whenever you can,
offer your support to the sick, the needy,
the vulnerable, the dispossessed,
the frightened, and the aged.

People sometimes need a shoulder to cry
on, or another soul to help them
in their hours of darkness.

Sympathise and empathise with those
who are feeling lonely,
with those who are in grief,
and with those who are in pain.

Think of others who are in distress at this
time, then contact them or visit them,
and help them.

Pray for them;
and have a sympathetic heart.

Your world will change for the better
when you change your Self.

"I realise now that I need to be healed," said the old Traveller, as he rested his aching bones on a seat of rock. His frail body was now a burden to him because the years had weathered it and dulled its ability to do his bidding as he would have liked.

Weary of his pilgrimage, he supported his aged frame with his gnarled hands at either side of him, and listened for a response.

But nothing came...

"I am in need of solace and healing," his voice quavered again.

But Silence fell all around him.

Then a loving whisper of encouragement entered his spirit, as if carried on a gentle breeze:

It is in the healing
that you are healed.

Surely, now is the time to heal
the hearts of those whom your words
and deeds have wronged?

Then quite suddenly the powerful voice of a
Shining Angel of Wisdom cried out mightily
from the mountaintops on high:

Don't cloak your Light –
let everyone see it!

All Light-workers are given spiritual
knowledge and power to pass them on to
people who are ignorant of The Truth.

Spread the good word far and wide.

Tell everyone your good news.

Do good works.

Set up or join a network of
spiritually-minded people who will
dedicate themselves to enlightening
mankind, and to freeing him
from the darkness of ignorance.

Light-workers are educators
who understand that knowledge is power;
and the powerful healing thought
that motivates them is:
service;
service;
service.

If you walk in The Light
your heart is lit.

If you breathe in The Light
your soul is filled with radiance.

When you live in The Light
you become The Light,
and its rays will then shine out
to relieve others of their darkness,
and heal them.

Your soul
draws its life-energies from
The Powerful Spirit of God,
and from deep within your heart
etheric healing rays radiate
as you go through the process
of living a thoughtful life.

Your thoughts and actions
are expressions of Light,
which is instantly replenished
by The Living Sun
that will never go out.

And the more you express
The Healing Light of Love,
the brighter your Soul will become,
and the greater will be your happiness
in The Everlasting Kingdom.

Realise that The Light of Hope is never
extinguished, it is only dimmed a little.

There is always Hope – it never dies.

Even when situations occur that seem
entirely devoid of relief,
do not be deceived – Hope is present.

Hope's flame can be fanned and
encouraged by you until it burns so
brightly that it illuminates and heals
all within the house,
and no corner is left in darkness.

The Children of The Darkness
  fear The Children of The Light,
   for The Light
    reveals their shadowed hearts...

Go then into The Darkness
  all you Children of The Light,
    and bring to Life the hearts of men...

Traveller,
in order to be healthy and happy
you must balance The Light in your
triune nature.

Happiness and contentment are
mental outlooks: they are states of mind.

Widen your outlook,
and brighten it.

People who seek happiness solely through
the possession of material objects
(and this includes 'owning'
a loving partner)
may search for it in vain;
for all material things are transient –
they will pass away.

Be a spiritually minded person.

Let reconciliation and co-operation
be your watchwords.

Steer the ship of your life into
calm and peaceful waters,
and do your best to avoid
the tempestuous seas of anger,
hostility and resentment.

Be the one who quells the storms that
rage all around you
and within you.

Bring a healing spirit of agreement
into your home and family.

Be the person who is courageous enough
to make the first move to repair
splintering relationships,
and to encourage warring factions to
make peace with each other.

Seek reconciliation, always.

And do not forget that some of the best
healing vibrations are produced by
laughter and fun,
and by a good sense of humour.

Use these vibrations often;
but never use sarcasm
at another person's expense.

To be whole and healthy,
you should settle old disagreements
amicably, and remove any thorns of
bitterness from your mind,
thereby cleansing your spirit.

You are the one who must start this
healing process; do not leave it to others.

Take right-action now,
and try to resolve your differences.

Remember that an outward-looking soul
is much healthier and happier
than an inward-looking one.

Take your mind off yourself,
and do something positive to help
the planet, or your loved ones
in this world
or in the next,
and you will experience greater fulfilment
and calmness, within.

Healthy is the man who is patient
with himself and others.

Through patient self-examination you
can attain peacefulness of mind and
then radiate these healing vibrations to
others who find themselves in turmoil.

Recognise that you have earned
the privilege of being a human being,
and let your soul sing.

Tune your soul to
The Master Healing Musician –
sing out your unique song
and heal yourself.

It does not matter if no one else joins in
with you – it's your song,
so sing it and be happy to be alive.

Singing is a healing and health-giving
exercise that creates regenerating
energy-vibrations
all around you and within you.

Open your soul and sing.

Sing something every day.

Surround yourself
with pleasant music and
with bright and pleasing colours.

Do not live in dark and drab
surroundings.

Colour your life with radiant hues
and you will benefit from the hidden
healing energies that they will project
into your mind.

Immerse yourself in
happy thoughts and circumstances,
and these psychic vibrations will lift up
your spirits and feed your soul
with positive life-energies.

And do not neglect to heal the world
all around you.

Nurture and care for the planet,
The Great Mother Earth,
upon which you live and move,
and have your being.

Do not poison her veins and flesh with
harmful chemicals, or waste her precious
resources – cherish her
and protect her as you would shield
the pupils of your own eyes.

And this is the real healing miracle:

If you but ask,
The Great Spirit will bless you
and your loved ones
with
The Peace that passes understanding,
with The Spiritual Truth
that will set you free,
and with The Light of Love
that will heal all sorrow and distress.

"I'm very old, now, but hopefully a little wiser,"
thought the elderly Traveller, resting again for a
moment. "And I think I've discovered my God,
and understood His Mighty Will. I shall soon
be finished with the Earth and all its pleasure
and pain. Surely now, Great Master, I can
open the doors to any world that I choose?"
And a gentle but ancient spirit rebuked him,
saying:

Who among you has the power to prevent
or delay by one second the Will of God?
Not one of you.
God's Will
will be done.
God holds All The Keys.
Therefore, strengthen your awareness of
His Presence in your life.
Man believes himself to be sophisticated
and intelligent, yet he can only stand and
marvel at the awesome
and absolute power displayed by
The Almighty One.

You ask where can you find the Father
and His Kingdom?

Look into the eyes of a child,
and you will see Him there.
Glance at a crimson sunset,
and He is there.
In the perfume and beauty
of a perfect flower you will discover
your Maker's Presence.

In the natural world, in space,
in your mind, in every form
and in every one of your thoughts –
The Father and His Kingdom are there.
Expand your mind and sense Him.
He lives within His people: stretch out
your hands and touch Him – then heal
His Children with a tender caress.

Embrace the God of All Healing lovingly,
and His Mind will guide you aright.

God's Spirit contains everything
that ever was,
that is now,
and that ever will be.

God is not simply Love, alone.

The word 'evil' describes some of
The Darker Forces that are living within
The Spirit of God.

The All keeps Itself
in Perfect Balance:
one act of positive kindness
is perpetrated for each act of seemingly
negative cruelty.

God is an evolving Spirit.

The Creator
is a Living and Progressing Spirit
whose personality is perhaps most evident
in Nature, where life-forms are
continually created and then destroyed
(sometimes by cataclysmic forces)
only to be later reconstituted
into new creations.

There is a birth, a life, and a death;
and then there is a rebirth
into an Eternal World of Light.

Everything has a beginning,
a middle,
and an end.

God is moving through your actions.

In this new day, reflect upon how your
character has grown
and you will take a positive step
towards spiritual progression.

It is in the understanding of
what you have done to others,
and of what they have done to you,
that you will come to know your Self
as you truly are.

Everything that you are
and all that you do
has been brought about by
an aspect of The Great Flame
for one purpose only –
so that It may burn brighter,
so that It may evolve
Its Consciousness.

The Great Reality
is constantly recycling Itself,
and It has the Power
not only to Create and to Sustain
but also to Transform or to Disintegrate
all Life-forms.

Aspects of your own life follow this same
sequence of events.

But adversity will not defeat you
because The Unknowable will give you
the knowledge,
the strength
and the intelligence
to overcome all of your trials.

You can either respect God,
The Great River of Life,
and flow along within Its Power,
or suffer the consequences
of trying to battle upstream.

You are swimming through God;
and the happiest souls are those
who have learned to swim
with The Current.

Go with the flow of God.

Release your anxieties and
let go of all worries about your future,
and instead, allow yourself to be swept
along by the mighty tide of
God's Inspiration.

Don't battle against The Current.

God has set down a pattern for your life
and has given you the power to follow it.
Never worry and never fear, for you are
exactly where you are supposed to be,
and you are the person that you were
meant to be – and the conditions that you
are now experiencing were designed to
accelerate your spiritual progression.

Take bold strides forward.

Seeker of The Beloved,
you cannot love God and hate man.

You cannot praise God
and denigrate your neighbour.

You cannot be kind to God and be cruel to
a tree, a bird, an animal,
or any other life-form.

You cannot worship God and spit out
bitterness and guile at others.

God is in Man: God is in all things.
He is your neighbour:
He is the tree, the bird, the animal,
and All that Is around you.

Respect everything and everyone,
for in so doing you are respecting God —
and if you respect God,
God will respect you.

God is The First Cause,
and The Last Effect.

There is only One Power in the Universe,
and nothing can exist outside
this Power of Consciousness,
outside this Great One.

Therefore, because this Spirit is present
in every personality
that It has ever created,
the 'Personality' of God can be discovered
everywhere, and in every thing.

Recognise that God is a Power,
and not a glorified human being,
and you will realise that your difficulties
arise from your dealings with other souls.

God can be seen in the workings of
the living world around you,
and also in the spiritual and psychic
worlds within you.

The Power is within you.

'Nature is red in tooth and claw' only
because parts of The Great Spirit are still
struggling to evolve through it,
still trying to progress towards
the state of Perfect Love.

Because your Cosmic Parent
loves you unconditionally,
He has placed all the answers
within you.

Associate yourself more with
the lights of love and compassion,
and less with the darker forces
of hatred and 'evil' –
for this is the road of evolution
along which God's Spirit is travelling.

And do not raise any man or woman
to the status of God:
do not deify any creature,
for this is a profane action.

The higher you build up a soul,
the further it will eventually fall;
and in the end you will disappoint
the object of your affections,
and you will disillusion yourself.

Try to understand that when people
commit heinous or anti-social acts,
some of the negative and
less-evolved parts of God's Spirit are
expressing themselves in despicable ways.

But it is the duty
of the more-evolved parts of God's Spirit
to encourage these struggling entities
to develop and express the power of
compassion in their lives.

Through witnessing your shining
example of giving love to all,
they will eventually learn to become
purer in heart.

You should always acknowledge
the presence of Hope
among the ashes of Despair.

In the innocent eyes of a child
God and His Universe
and all its wonders are contained.

Look again, then, with simple eyes,
and see the glory in the dust.

Smile, and start afresh.

No mountain is too high to climb
and no ocean is too deep to fathom,
for with God's aid
the impossible can be achieved.

Petition Him lovingly,
and if whatever you request will benefit
your soul, or the souls of others —
your prayers will surely be granted.

But what transpires
will be dictated by The Universal Laws,
and not by man;
for God is All-seeing,
and His plans stretch much further into
the future than yours do.

Speak to God as if to a friend, a mother,
a lover, or a child; as if to someone or
to some beloved creature
that you care for deeply.

Do not approach God with angry
thoughts, for like attracts like,
and The Creator responds likewise.

Be gentle in your requests,
but be sincere — and do your best to feel
His Presence within your spirit.

If you are not sensitive enough to be
aware of The Living Presence of God's
Ministering Angels around you,
or of His Own Spirit within you,
then simply trust that all is well.

Have faith, and know that He is
fully aware of your circumstances.

You cannot command God to do
your bidding.

Neither is it within your power to
direct completely the pathway of
any other creature.

You would be better
employed giving more time and thought
to your own pathway.

Ask for sensible guidance to reach you.

And when you need to pray,
pray in this manner:
close your eyes and ears; shut out the
physical world and enter into the realm of
your mind.
Stop your thoughts from galloping
uncontrollably – rein them in
and silence them.
Speak gently to your Maker in word or
thought and He will hear you;
He will listen.

His Ministers will judge your words,
your needs and your desires, and they
will grant whatever you truly need
in order to fulfil your destiny and to
outwork the reasons for your incarnation.

But the conditions that will be brought
about as a result of your spontaneous
prayer may not necessarily be what you
yourself would desire.

And do not trouble God with problems
that you can deal with yourself.

Do your best to sort out your own life.

Turn to God only when you can do no
more for yourself, or when the cause of
your difficulties is so far distant from you
that you need His extra power
to bring about a significant change.

And when next you wonder
"Am I treading the right pathway?"

Remember that the answer is:
Yes, you are.

There is only one pathway
that is uniquely right for you,
and you are now walking it.

Birth into the Earthworld
'locks' each soul
into a set of circumstances
designed to provide it with opportunities
for growth.

At present, if the purpose of your Life
eludes you, do not be concerned,
for the purpose is surely there.

The pathway was set down long ago
in a World of Light where you existed
as an individual in another dimension.

You undertook to live this particular life
and to experience all of its joys and pains.

Sometimes the Way seems clear to you,
but at other times the road seems dark
and thickly lined with fog.

Nevertheless,
you will walk forward into your destiny.

Life is an adventure
in which there will be times of great joy,
exploration, revelation, and excitement,
counterbalanced by times of introspection,
sadness and quietness of thought.

Your life is an exciting odyssey —
marvel at what each new day brings.

And remember that it is not what
happens to you that matters,
what counts is how you deal with it.

Life is all about growth and expansion,
about unfolding
your sensitivity and awareness,
and about gaining experience.

Day follows night and the seasons roll:
spring follows winter — in a similar
fashion, happiness, sadness, joy, love,
despair, hardship and ecstasy,
and the whole gamut of human
experiences are provided by God
so that you may spiritually evolve.

Welcome your experiences, therefore,
and learn from them — then step forward
into the next adventure.

Like a great river, Life flows unceasingly:
sometimes the waters move
in frantic torrents,
and at other times they glide along slowly
and peacefully — but they can still surprise
you by twisting around unexpected bends.

Whether you like it or not,
the river's invisible current will always
carry you forward;
it can never take you backwards;
and not one of us can control or command
The Tide.
We are for ever at the mercy of
The Current.

And the river was flowing in full spate
long before human beings were created,
and aeons before sentient creatures
sprouted limbs and learned how to swim.

Traveller:
you are marching forward.
You cannot turn back the clock and change
what has happened –
though you can learn from it.

But how can you face your future
with open arms
if you are still clutching on to your past?

You cannot.

Let go of your 'failures'.

Release your hurts and
turn away from the past
and face the future with open arms –
and embrace it.

If your life distresses you:
temporarily remove yourself from
your circumstances and, for a while,
do something new or different.

Create a new thought-pattern.

Then, when you return to your
responsibilities,
they will seem easier to bear.

Seeker:
bear your trials with fortitude.

No one escapes life's difficulties:
everyone must conquer them boldly.

And whenever sadness touches your heart,
remember that buried deep within your
soul there is an Infinite Depth of
Spiritual Love,
an Infinite Supply of Psychic Strength
upon which you may draw.

This Great Well of
The Living Spirit's Power
will never run dry,
and It will help you to win through.

If you sometimes feel that you have lost
your way, or think that your days seem
meaningless, be assured of this:

Spiritually, you are never lost —
and the pathway that your soul
agreed to tread before it came into this
world will unfold before your eyes,
step by step,
moment by moment,
day by day,
year by year.

You must live the life that
you were born to live.

And you will forever move forward into
new ground.

Tomorrow will bring a new day
with a whole new raft of feelings
and a wealth of new realisations.

Today, if you are troubled:
sleep on your problems.

Your mind works in symbols, pictures,
thoughts and feelings, so try to be more
aware of the images that you experience,
and then interpret them as best you can.

By all means glance back,
for your history has brought you to where
you are today; and in the looking back
you may more clearly see
the way forward.

But do not wish your life away
in fanciful dreams and schemes:
'If only...' is a waste of energy.

See your life as it is:
look it straight in the eye
and you will be able to face it
bravely.

Pilgrim on the Road:

Breathe in The Breath of God
and Live Life's Adventure
to the full.

5.

The Voice of Eternity is calling…

And the ancient Traveller, now barely able to stand, and feeling world-weary and nearing the end of his days, came to the far end of the Valley of Wisdom and stood shakily before a vast wall of misty Golden Light, and he thought, "This must be The World of the Soul... The end is near... my heartbeat grows faint, and it is time to say farewell to the Earth and all that is in it. But I'm not sorry to go, for I have lived long enough.

"Great God of All Things, my body is tired and its energies are spent... I will sleep now, and release my spirit into your safekeeping... for it is finished. My journey is over..."

But a Silent Watcher called his name, and corrected him, saying:

Your journey is just beginning,
and no one can halt at the gate
when the hour is at hand.
Do not be afraid...

Child of The Living God:
Step forward, into The Light...

And the old Traveller moved out of his body
and glided into immediate Peace and
Radiance – and momentarily he found
himself between Two Worlds, in a place of
Light where time seemed to have no meaning;
and the spiritual voices continued to reassure
him, saying:

Eternal Life is granted to everyone,
irrespective of his or her beliefs:
it is the natural birthright of all souls.

Life is Everlasting.

You are a Divine Being clothed in flesh,
an Immortal Soul powered by
an Infinite Spirit expressing Itself
through a temporary physical shell.

The Great Spirit is Eternal,
and so are you.

Your body is finite,
but your soul is Infinite.

You will live for ever.

There will never be a death for your Spirit;
and because of this Law
new opportunities will be
presented to you, endlessly.

You can always start again:
you can rethink your plan of action
and you can recommence
your tasks.

Earth is but a fleeting dream,
faint shadows cast
by Greater Lights Beyond:

only The Essence
may know The Source;

only The Soul
maps out The Way;

and your Spirit is for ever
in touch with Eternity...

Voyager, have no fear:
there is no death, and there are no dead.

Those you have 'lost'
are nearer to you now than your own
hands and feet, and you will see them.

You have mourned for your loved ones
but these beloved souls
are now progressing in The Light;
and in an eye-blink,
as you would gauge time,
you will meet them again.

It matters not that there is no
marriage-bond in The Kingdom of Light:
there will still be a glorious reunion
because true love will always claim
its own.

For true love, like God, is Eternal,
and it is stronger than death.

And death is not a tragedy to
those who die.

Death is not an end but a beginning;
but there will be many 'little deaths'
along the Way.

Die, then, to your past,
Voyager,
and be reborn now to a brighter future.

Traveller at The Gate:
throughout your life
there have been some tearful partings
and some sad goodbyes.

But bereavement comes not only when
you lose a special soul through the death
of the body: you can feel bereaved when
a cause is lost
or when a plan is thwarted.

Trouble comes to every family,
and none can escape it.
Tragedy touches every soul on Earth,
without exception.

But grief teaches us that we are not in
total control of our lives —
we must bow to a Greater Power.

Somewhere along life's journey,
all souls must learn acceptance;
and all souls must adopt a degree of
resignation to The Will of God,
and engender within themselves
a willingness to let go of the Self.

Traveller:
you can own nothing in the material
world, because you are only a steward.

You stand now between Two Worlds —
the Earthworld and the many dimensions
of The Spirit World, in which there are
many planes of thought
and many worlds within worlds,
within worlds,
within which you may live.

But no one stands alone.

No one is neglected or unwanted.

No one is unwatched or unguided.

Every one is cherished by
The One Whose Love is Inexhaustible.

And nothing has ever been hidden
or been kept secret from Him —
all is known.

He sees you now as you truly are.

You who are finite physical beings,
cannot possibly comprehend
The Power of The Infinite Being.

Its Universe is vast
and there is life in it that man
has not yet discovered.

There are forms of life that are well in
advance of man's development,
and there are life-forms that are not so
advanced as man is.

Because it is impossible for you to know
all things in such an immense
Theatre of Life — spurn arrogance, always,
and embrace humility...

And do not forget that your actions on
Earth will determine your place in
The Eternal World,
because in The Spirit Planes
the 'good' and the 'cruel'
cannot inhabit the same Sphere of Life.

There is no deathbed repentance that can
change a man filled with cruelty and
unkindness into a radiant soul
filled with love.

You are what you are,
and you will change only through
your own efforts and hard work
throughout Eternity.

There is no cheating
The Ever-Loving Mind.

And even though, at times, you may feel
unloved or quite alone,
you will never be lonely,
for you are surrounded by
Beings of Light
and by the spirit-forms of those
beloved ones who birthed you,
helped you, supported you,
and cared for you for many years.

They care for you still,
and they surround you now
in The Silence.

Have no fear:
solitude is good for your soul.
Quieten your mind and spirit
and listen for their guidance…

Do not be afraid of The Silence –
welcome it.

In solitude and quiet reflection, you can
obtain power, light, inspiration,
angelic help, and a wonderful sense of
Inner Divine Peace.

In solitude,
and in prayer,
you can energise your personal power.

Voyager:
in the times that lie ahead —
regularly embrace The Silence
and feed your soul with Power and Light.

And never complain that
"Nothing happens in the silence,"
for major spiritual development often
takes place in the quietness, when
invisible intelligences draw near to you
and learn to attune their minds to
your Higher Self.

Those who lovingly embrace The Silence
and listen to it very carefully
will soon discover
that it is full of sound...

Traveller:
the common link that binds you to
the many souls in The Eternal World
is the very Spirit that is within you; and
because of this everlasting magnetic link
a line of guidance will remain
forever open to you.

Whenever you need help,
communicate telepathically with
your Group-Souls,
with your Spiritual Guardians,
and they will come to your assistance.

Seek and you will find –
but remember:
you have an Eternity in which to
discover your true purpose.

Meditate regularly
and suggest to your mind that it
may like to daydream a little,
for all Travellers need to spend some time
in gentle contemplation.

And suddenly a Profound Peace and Stillness
swept into the Traveller's Soul on his short
journey between The Two Worlds, and with it
came a gentle voice that read his concerns
about those he might meet on The Other Side
of The Veil, and it said:

Everyone survives death intact,
irrespective of whether they believe this
or not.

All souls, including the souls of
unborn children and animals,
will survive the grave,
complete with their minds and characters,
no matter how the transition is taken;
and you will eventually meet them all.

The Spiritual Kingdoms are ruled by
The Power of Thought,
and life on Earth prepares everyone
for their existence in Eternity.

The Gateway is open to All.

And know this:
all the paths that souls have trodden,
all the ways that they have taken,
all the diversions that they have
encountered, and may encounter again,
have always been
clearly mapped out.

So it is with every life.

Traveller at The Gate,
you can possess a body, a house, a job,
a reputation, an opinion, desires,
dreams, hopes, and expectations —
but none of these are permanent.

Only you
will last for ever.

Priorities must be put into perspective.

The characteristics that matter are:
what you think and what you do,
for these colour the way in which you
behave toward other life-forms;
and it is this conduct that will
immediately gravitate your spirit body
towards souls of your own kind
in your future Sphere of Life in Eternity —
and this Judgement is automatic,
and unequivocal.

You will earn your place in The Beyond.

And if you feel you have not achieved your
purpose in this incarnation,
the opportunity may present itself to you
to tackle your tasks again —
because you have plenty of time
ahead of you,
and eternal progress is open to all souls.

Do not be fooled into thinking that you
are a being who is governed by Time –
for you are not.

Your mind and soul are timeless,
and you are living in Timelessness
right now.

The idea of the past, the present, and
the future belongs to the Earthplane only.

In the Great Scheme of Everlasting Life,
This Moment only
is the important one.

Because you are living
in the Ever-present Now,
simply move through this space,
learning from your experiences
as you go.

There are spiritual reasons operating
behind everything that occurs,
but you are passing through these
experiences, and then passing on...

And when the moment comes for
the silver cord to dematerialise, and for
you to vacate your body of flesh and to
cross over into The Spirit Realms
in your Inner Body of Light,
do you think you will be equipped to
live there happily; or will you arrive
mentally and spiritually bankrupt?

Again we tell you:
your future happiness is decided by
your outlook and your conduct when you
lived upon the Earth:
by the development of your loving heart,
by the depth, expansion, wisdom, and
openness contained within in your mind,
and by your efforts to question,
to reason, to care,
and to serve.

Travellers all:
you are Immortal Souls upon
The Road of Spiritual Progression.

At the appointed time
you moved out of Freedom
and into Restriction —
but back into Freedom
your souls must fly...

Pilgrim upon Life's Pathway:
know that in Eternity
your Conscience will be more highly
sensitive to your memories,
and your thoughts will shape your
surroundings.

The Voice of your Conscience,
which is The Divine Monitor,
will motivate you to make redress
and to serve those
whom you may have wronged.

Voyager,
you have travelled a long road.

Glance back now into your past and
compare your behaviour then with the
way in which you behave now.

Great strides forward can be made after
a little introspection and reflection.

Examine your character to see if you have
yet attained the priceless spiritual
qualities of Forgiveness,
Reconciliation,
and Unconditional Love...

For when you reach The Next World,
remember that what you have professed to
believe will be of little account
when measured against
what you have actually done
in your Earthlife.

In The Light,
you will be known as you truly are.

For everything that you think, say, and do,
is registered upon the fabric of your soul
and recorded in your mind.

It is time now to move forward...

And the silver cord broke, and the old Traveller made his transition quite effortlessly.

Leaving behind him the body of pain and inheriting a body of energy, he moved swiftly through the brilliant Guide-Star, and into The Golden Light – and he discovered he was young again: refreshed and renewed, and full of health and vigour in his New World.

Stunned by the sensation of lightness, his spirit thanked His God for the very Gift of Life; and then he was overwhelmed by the arrival of his family and by the many other dear souls he had loved and thought he had lost – "But now I have found you again!"

Crying with joy, he embraced them lovingly... then smiled and promised, "My friends, I will speak with you all again soon." And then he found himself somewhere in the deepness of space, glancing behind him at the spinning orb of The Great Mother, and realised that he, himself, had now become a spiritual voice that could communicate with the Earth – so he opened his mind and transmitted thoughtfully to The Children of The Blue Planet:

from the place where stars
   are born and die
      comes the light that infuses
         the mind of man;

from the centre of the heart
   of a cosmic soul
      comes the breath of life
         which beats in all;

from the furthest stretch
   beyond universal space
      comes the shadow of a future now;

from the tiniest speck
   of planetary dust
      comes a world as yet unknown;

from the middle of the human spirit
   springs eternal life...

And rejoicing he called out again to those
billions of Travelling Souls who were still
encased in the flesh, struggling to attain a
degree of happiness, and still wondering if there
was Peace at the end of the Road:

And
when we stand
on the Shores of Eternity
and look back
upon our Experiences
in Earthlife,
we will notice
how all the things we did
happened
in just the right places,
at just the right times:

and
we shall say to Ourselves:

It is Good.

If you enjoyed this psychic book,
then you will enjoy reading Stephen O'Brien's
other bestselling titles,
and also listening to his acclaimed
spiritual and psychic teachings
recorded on audio cassettes.

Books are available through all good Bookstores
and Libraries everywhere;
and signed Cassettes and Books are available from
the Voices Mail Order Service,
or via the Internet from
the Voices Online Shop at:
www.stephenobrien.co.uk

Full details, and a contact address for Stephen,
appear on the following pages.

'VISIONS OF ANOTHER WORLD'
The Autobiography of Medium,
by Stephen O'Brien.

Every Journey has a Beginning…

Phantom hands hammering on a door
in the dead of night:
THE SPIRIT WORLD WAS CALLING…
and Stephen O'Brien had to accept the remarkable powers
that brought him *Visions of Another World*.

Then the tragic early death of his mother broke his
life in two; but miraculously she appeared to him
from beyond the grave
and her love changed the course of his life:
he became a Medium and a Visionary.
He promised the soul of a long-dead American Indian
that he would serve the Spirit World,
and countless thousands packed out venues
to hear him relay messages of Hope,
Light and Survival
from their loved ones on the Other Side of Life.
Hundreds of thousands of the so-called 'dead' have now
communicated through Stephen O'Brien's
amazing gifts: including war heroes,
accident and murder victims,
innocent children who died too young, animals,
and even the world-famous actress, Judy Garland.

Now you can read Stephen's compelling life-story.

'Big powers in other-worldly communication
and healing' *Irish News*

A Voices Paperback (384 pages; illustrated)
ISBN: 0-953-6620-3-9

'ANGELS BY MY SIDE'
The Psychic Life of a Medium,
by Stephen O'Brien.

'We are not alone in this Universe…'

Stephen O'Brien's extraordinary spiritual and
psychic gifts have comforted millions of people and
have silenced sceptics around the world.
In *Angels By My Side* Stephen reveals through his
acclaimed powers:

♦ Timeless Wisdom from the 'Silent Sentinels'
 and Angel Beings who watch over us.

♦ Fascinating glimpses into Mankind's Future.

♦ The secret Psychic Powers of Light and Colour that
 enhance Wellbeing and Self-healing.

♦ A compelling view of 'The One Living God'.

♦ What kind of life awaits us all after death,
 and the secrets of the Next World.

♦ Irrefutable Evidence of Survival.

He also shares with his countless readers
more of his amazing Out-of-the-Body Excursions
into the Spirit World itself.

A Voices Paperback (384 pages; illustrated)
ISBN: 0-953-6620-0-4

'IN TOUCH WITH ETERNITY'
Contact with Another World,
by Stephen O'Brien.

> *'As the hazy shape materialised*
> *there was revealed to us an Angel of Light,*
> *a beautiful woman with golden hair,*
> *whose eyes were deep blue-green like*
> *unfathomed ocean waters.*
> *"Peace," she said...'*

Make incredible journeys into the World of the Spirit
with Stephen O'Brien's remarkable
True-Life Psychic Experiences:

Go behind the scenes at Séances and discover how
Guardian Angels strive to contact us through the
Psychic Power that we unknowingly provide.
Read stunning Survival Evidence of human and
animal souls after death, including children's
messages to their parents and a communication
from Dr Martin Luther King.

♦ Unveil the truth about Reincarnation,
  Telepathy, Life Before Life,
  Out-of-the-Body Experiences,
  Soul Powers, and how to Heal with Psychic Sound.
♦ Encounter *'The Shining Ones'* deep within the
  Spiritual Spheres of Light, and learn of their
  concern for the human family and for our planet.
♦ Meet the Nature Spirits, and some amazing
  Animals that can communicate with us.

A Host of Fascinating Spiritual Experiences
from Britain's Renowned Visionary,
Medium and Healer.

A Voices Paperback (352 pages; illustrated)
ISBN: 0-953-6620-2-0

'VOICES FROM HEAVEN'
Communion with Another World
by Stephen O'Brien

Grieving parents are reunited with their children,
wives with their husbands, and even animals return
to prove what medium Stephen O'Brien affirms:
'Death is only an Illusion.'

Follow Stephen as he makes remarkable journeys
into the Realms of Light and discovers the Eternal
World of the Spirit that awaits us all after 'death'.
In these fascinating psychic recollections
the world-renowned visionary reveals to his countless
followers many remarkable life-changing and spiritual
experiences, during which he:

❖ Crosses Time-Zones and meets people who are
long-dead.
❖ Relays startling messages from screen goddess
Marilyn Monroe, from Lord Olivier, and from
Earl Mountbatten of Burma.
❖ Foresees the *Challenger* Space Shuttle disaster,
an incredible five years before it happened.
❖ Provides irrefutable evidence of the immortality
of the soul.

*

And the Angel's Voice said:
'The road is never spiritually lonely,
and we will not forsake you.
We will guide and bless you, for ever...'

'The epitome of mediumistic excellence' –
Psychic News

A Voices Paperback (384 pages; illustrated)
ISBN: 0-953-6620-4-7

'A GIFT OF GOLDEN LIGHT'
The Psychic Journeys of a Medium,
by Stephen O'Brien:

The press described this remarkable book as
'un-put-downable'.

Follow Stephen as he recalls his exciting 20-year
psychic apprenticeship and strives to perfect the extraordinary
paranormal skills which have brought happiness,
comfort and hope to millions of people.
With warmth and candour he:

◆ Shares his thrilling encounters with Apparitions, Hauntings,
  Spiritual Healing and Telepathic Powers.
◆ Reveals the mystical Gift of Golden Light which
  illuminates everyone's Spiritual Journey through Life.
◆ Presents a compelling array of Survival Evidence of Human
  and Animal Souls after death.

'Stunning clairvoyance… superb mediumship' –
Psychic News

*(If you are interested in developing your own psychic or
spiritual powers, simply by reading this book you will learn all
the important lessons and guidelines that Stephen learned
during his long apprenticeship.)*

A Voices Paperback (384 pages; illustrated)
ISBN: 0-9536620-1-2

*Available from our worldwide Mail Order
service, or you may order these titles through
good bookstores and libraries everywhere,
or Online through Internet outlets. Signed copies are
available from the Voices Online Shop in the vast
spiritual teachings website at:* www.stephenobrien.co.uk

Keep in touch with our mail order department for news of new
titles and other products originated by Stephen.

For further information on all aspects of the
life and work of visionary, spiritual healer,
medium and poet, Stephen O'Brien,
including how to obtain by Mail Order
his bestselling books, educational cassettes,
spiritual healing crystals, and a full range of
other quality products (or to contact him directly)
please write, enclosing a large SAE, to:

VOICES MANAGEMENT
(Dept VB6)
PO Box 8
SWANSEA
SA1 1BL
UK

Or search the Internet for 'Stephen O'Brien'.
Visit our Online Shop where you may order signed
copies of all of the Stephen O'Brien products at:
www.stephenobrien.co.uk

Voices Management regrets it cannot reply
without a large stamped self-addressed envelope
and correspondents are respectfully advised
not to mail irreplaceable items to the author,
for neither Voices, nor Mr O'Brien,
can accept responsibility for the loss or damage
of any unsolicited manuscripts, poems,
sentimental objects, photographs, or cassettes etc.,
which are often posted by the public.
Your letters are always welcome,
but please keep them brief and to the point –
and be patient when awaiting your replies,
for Stephen receives vast quantities of mail
from around the world.

Thank you.